EXPERIENCING
Spiritual
GROWTH

Focus on the Family

Gospel Light

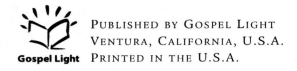

PUBLISHED BY GOSPEL LIGHT
VENTURA, CALIFORNIA, U.S.A.
PRINTED IN THE U.S.A.

Gospel Light is a Christian publisher dedicated to serving the local church. We believe God's vision for Gospel Light is to provide church leaders with biblical, user-friendly materials that will help them evangelize, disciple and minister to children, youth and families.

It is our prayer that this Gospel Light resource will help you discover biblical truth for your own life and help you minister to others. May God richly bless you.

For a free catalog of resources from Gospel Light, please call your Christian supplier or contact us at 1-800-4-GOSPEL *or* www.gospellight.com.

PUBLISHING STAFF
William T. Greig, Chairman · **Dr. Elmer L. Towns,** Senior Consulting Publisher · **Pam Weston,** Editor · **Jessie Minassian,** Assistant Editor · **Bayard Taylor, M.Div.,** Senior Editor, Biblical and Theological Issues · **Rosanne Moreland,** Cover and Internal Designer · **Jessie Minassian,** Contributing Writer

ISBN 0-8307-3365-5
© 2005 Focus on the Family
All rights reserved.
Printed in the U.S.A.

contents

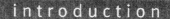
EXPERIENCING SPIRITUAL GROWTH

But the fruit of the Spirit is love, joy, peace, patience, kindness, goodness,
faithfulness, gentleness and self-control. Against such things there is no law.

GALATIANS 5:22-23

There was once a woman who decided to plant a garden. After hours of weeding, mulching and watering the soil, she dug little holes with her fingertips and carefully planted the tiny seeds. She watered the garden each afternoon, anxiously peering into the muddy soil so that she wouldn't miss the arrival of the first tiny shoots. Several days passed, but the woman still didn't see any green seedlings. *What if they don't grow?* she began to wonder. *Perhaps I didn't water them enough, or maybe the sun is too hot. Oh, I hope the seeds didn't get eaten!*

The impatient woman related her dilemma to a friend, who replied, "Oh, don't worry, plants *want* to grow. That's what God made them to do! You just keep watering those seeds, and before you know it, you'll have your garden."

A few days passed. The woman was faithful to water the garden, though she still peered anxiously into the soil each afternoon. Sure enough, the little seeds began to surface, thrust upward by sturdy green stems. The woman was delighted! She would have her garden after all because seeds *want* to grow.

Spiritual growth in a believer's life is similar to the seeds in this story. When we are faithful to water the seeds of our faith by practicing spiritual disciplines, the fruit of the Spirit is destined to grow. Much of the growth appears under the surface. Like the woman, we may be tempted to question whether any growth is taking place at all! But rest assured, a believer is *designed* to grow. All we have to do is add water!

Consider this study as a gardener's guide to watering the seeds of faith in your life to produce a rich spiritual harvest. Just like a physical garden, cultivating your spiritual life will take hard work and determination. The phrase "spiritual disciplines" is not a misnomer! The Holy Spirit will be there to play an instrumental role in perfecting His fruit in your life. He would like nothing more than to see the sweet fruit of love, joy, peace, patience, kindness, goodness, faithfulness, gentleness and self-control take root and blossom in your heart.

Note: This study is designed to show the correlation between the fruit of the Spirit and spiritual discipline in a believer's life. Because of this goal, we have not included all of the traditional spiritual disciplines.

FOCUS ON THE FAMILY'S WOMEN'S MINISTRY SERIES

And this is my prayer: that your love may abound more and more in knowledge and depth of insight, so that you may be able to discern what is best and may be pure and blameless until the day of Christ, filled with the fruit of righteousness that comes through Jesus Christ—to the glory and praise of God.

PHILIPPIANS 1:9-11

The goal of this series is to help women identify who they are, based on their unique nature and in the light of God's Word. We hope that each woman who is touched by this series will understand her heavenly Father's unfathomable love for her and that her life has a divine purpose and value. This series also has a secondary goal: That as women pursue their relationship with God, they will also understand the importance of building relationships with other women to enrich their own lives and grow personally, as well as to help others understand their God-given worth and purpose.

Session Overview

Experiencing Spiritual Growth can be used in a variety of situations, including small-group Bible studies, Sunday School classes or mentoring relationships.

An individual can also use this book as an at-home study tool.

Each session contains four main components.

Everyday Woman

This section introduces the topic for the session by giving you a personal glimpse into the life of an ordinary woman—someone you can relate to—and it asks probing questions to help you focus on the theme of the session.

Eternal Wisdom

This is the Bible study portion in which you will read Scripture and answer questions to help discover lasting truths from God's Word.

Enduring Hope

This section provides questions and commentary that encourage you to place your hope in God's plan.

Everyday Life

This is a time to reflect on ways that the Lord is calling you to change, suggesting steps you can take to get there. It is also a time for the whole group to pray and encourage one another.

Journaling

We encourage you to keep a journal while you are working through this study. A personal journal chronicles your spiritual journey, recording prayers, thoughts and events along the way. Reviewing past journal entries is a faith-building exercise that allows you to see how God has worked in your life—by resolving a situation, changing an attitude, answering your prayers or helping you grow more like Christ.

Leader's Discussion Guide

A leader's discussion guide is included at the end of this book to help leaders encourage participation, lead discussions and develop relationships.

There are additional helps for leading small groups or mentoring relationships in *The Focus on the Family Women's Ministry Guide.*

DEMONSTRATING *Love*

FELLOWSHIP

Let us consider how we may spur one another on toward love and good deeds.
Let us not give up meeting together, as some are in the habit of doing, but let us
encourage one another—and all the more as you see the Day approaching.
HEBREWS 10:24-25

The church is a community of believers who demonstrate genuine concern
for each other. Fellowship occurs, I believe, when there are expressions of
genuine Christianity freely shared among God's family members.
CHARLES SWINDOLL, *RISE AND SHINE*

EVERYDAY WOMAN

Alex immediately spotted the red van as she drove into the McKinley High School stadium parking lot. She felt guilty for parking in the section reserved for the visiting team, but she just couldn't handle seeing Kaitlyn—not today. Alex felt like her life wasn't in any shape for outside speculation. Today had been even more out of control than normal.

Alex had met Kaitlyn at one of her son's baseball team practices a few months ago. Alex thought it might be nice to get to know another mom from her son's team since she would be spending a lot of time in the stands over the course of the season. But once Kaitlyn found out that they attended the same church, the questions had started to fly. *Personal questions*, Alex had thought, *a little too personal.* Alex had only recently started attending church and was a relatively new Christian. *I guess I'm just not used to people invading my life with so much care and concern*, she reasoned. *I'm sure she means well.*

Today, despite Alex's attempts to fade into the crowd, Kaitlyn found her way over to Alex's side of the bleachers and plopped down beside her on the checkered blanket she always brought with her. Strangely, Alex felt almost relieved that Kaitlyn had found her.

"Hi, Alex! Some game, huh?"

"Yeah, it's a close one! Good to see you, Kaitlyn." Alex was surprised at how genuine she felt in saying it.

After some chit-chat about their children, Kaitlyn asked, "Have you had a chance to read that passage I gave you last week?"

Alex told her that she had and that she didn't quite understand what it meant. Kaitlyn patiently answered Alex's questions. As they talked, Alex's heart began to soften. *Lord*, she prayed silently, *thank You for sending someone who really cares about me and who isn't afraid of my dirty laundry. I have a feeling I really need Kaitlyn in my life.*[1]

Women are naturally relational creatures. We love get-togethers, long phone conversations, parties and socials. We thrive on relationships and look forward to spending time with our friends. God designed us for companionship. However, the discipline of fellowship is more than just spending time with each other—it's about creating meaningful, mutually beneficial relationships with our spiritual brothers and sisters that encourage us to become more like Christ.

1. Why do people often shy away from getting too close to others in relationships?

2. Why do you suppose Christians need to have close fellowship with other Christians?

3. In what ways has someone been an encouragement to you, showing you love and helping you grow in your relationship with Christ and with others?

At the very heart of the discipline of fellowship is one little word: "love."

ETERNAL WISDOM

Love is the root of all the fruit of the Spirit and spiritual disciplines. Why love? Wouldn't faith or obedience be a more logical fit? Let's explore God's Word for the answer.

4. In 1 John 4:16-17, how is God described?

God is love

What is the correlation between living in love and living in God?

Since "in this world we are all like him" (v. 17), what quality or characteristic should distinguish us from nonbelievers?

Confidence for the day of judgement - no fear.

Sounds easy enough, doesn't it? Not quite! Loving the way God loves is a tall order and completely impossible without the Holy Spirit living inside us. That's the beauty of living by the Spirit of God—all things become possible, including loving with a pure love.

5. Why is a pure love like God's a necessary element in Christian fellowship?

people are naturally skeptical & so pure love deminishes fear to get involved.

Loving others as God loves is necessary, but what does His kind of love look like? Let's investigate.

6. Read 1 Corinthians 13:4-8. Next to each of the following characteristics of love, give practical examples of how you might display these characteristics to others. You may want to use a dictionary, thesaurus, concordance and/or another Bible translation of this passage to help you form your ideas.

Patient – *Anna Kolesnichenko in line for money*

Kind – *going the 2nd mile without complaint*

Does not envy *No pouting when*

Does not boast *wait to be recognized for all accomplishment. Don't crow it out.*

Is not proud – *Ask for directions. Not a know-it-all.*

Is not rude – *speak kindly & patiently.*

Is not self-seeking *I'll do this and she'll be indebted to pay me back – No!*

Is not easily angered *even tempered, long fuse*

Keeps no record of wrongs - *forgets slights & acts the same.*

Does not delight in evil

Rejoices with the truth *glad when Righteousness prevails*

Protects

Trusts

Hopes - *positive*

Perseveres *Doesn't give up - Keeps going to finish a project.*

Never fails — *willing to keep trying*

7. Now read 1 Corinthians 13:13. Based on what you have learned about who God is and what His love looks like, why is love greater than hope and even faith? *It takes love at the center to be able to accomplish each one of the other things.*

8. As you read the following Scriptures, write after each reference what you learn about love.

John 13:34-35 *love is a distinguishing characteristic & requirement of being identified as a disciple of Jesus.*

Romans 13:10 *love fulfills the law by not doing wrong to a neighbor.*

1 Peter 4:8 *love covers a multitude of sins.*

1 John 4:12,20-21 *If you love God, you must love your brother*

Notice that the attributes of love in 1 Corinthians 13 are others oriented. They enable us to show genuine love to others in the context of Christian fellowship. However, fellowship also entails receiving genuine love from others. When God's children live in love, we all receive the benefits. Let's look at an example of this kind of fellowship.

9. In Acts 2:42-47, how did the believers exemplify the love described in 1 Corinthians 13 through their fellowship?

What physical, emotional and spiritual needs were met by their mutual love and fellowship?

What specific physical, emotional and spiritual needs do you have that could be met by true fellowship with other Christians?

ENDURING HOPE

In addition to the characteristics of love found in 1 Corinthians 13, God has given us another means to serve one another in Christian fellowship: spiritual gifts. These gifts are another by-product of walking by the Spirit. Although devoted, educated Christians differ in opinion regarding which gifts God still gives to Christians today, the purpose of these gifts is not generally debated.

10. According to 1 Corinthians 14:12, what purpose do spiritual gifts serve?

building up the church

11. Read the following list of spiritual gifts.[2] Place a check mark next to the spiritual gifts you feel that God has given you to bless others in the Body of Christ.

❑ Administration	❑ Knowledge
❑ Apostle	❑ Leadership
❑ Craftsmanship	❑ Mercy
❑ Discernment	❑ Miracles
❑ Evangelism	❑ Missionary
❑ Exhortation	❑ Music
❑ Faith	❑ Pastor/Teacher
❑ Giving	❑ Prophecy
❑ Healing	❑ Serving
❑ Helps	❑ Teaching
❑ Hospitality	❑ Wisdom
❑ Intercession	

Note: This list of spiritual gifts is by no means exhaustive. If you are interested in learning more about spiritual gifts and their functions, we recommend reading *Discover Your Spiritual Gifts* by C. Peter Wagner. To order *Discover Your Spiritual Gifts* or the self-scoring *Finding Your Spiritual Gifts Questionnaire*, please call your Christian supplier or contact Gospel Light at 1-800-4-GOSPEL or www.gospellight.com.

12. What other gifts, talents, attitudes and abilities has God given you to bless others in the Body of Christ?

God also gives us specific desires, dreams and passions to help us minister to His Body of believers. For example, if someone has a great love for children, she might offer to help in the nursery or to work as a volunteer at Vacation Bible School.

13. Complete each of the following statements regarding your passions:

I prefer to work with *babies*.

I am attracted to and have the greatest concern for
old ladies + college Age males.

My deepest desire is to make a difference in the following area:
my grandchildren

If money, time, family and education were not an issue, and knew I could not fail, I would

14. Based on your answers to questions 11 through 13, in what area(s) do you feel God may be calling you to serve the Body of Christ?

15. Do you feel you have been using your spiritual gifts and passions to their full potential? If not, in what ways can you begin to exercise those gifts for the sake of the Body of Christ?

If you feel you have been using your spiritual gifts as God intends, what benefits have you noticed others receive? What benefits have you received?

God is very intentional about the spiritual gifts, abilities and passions He gives to each of us. He has made each member of His Body unique so that our fellowship can be meaningful, fulfilling and mutually beneficial.

E V E R Y D A Y   L I F E

Knowing our spiritual gifts, abilities and passions is the first step, but we can't stop there. In our hectic lives it is easy to become so busy that we fail to make time for genuine fellowship. Some of us get so caught up in *serving* the Body that our relationships become superficial and our personal needs get neglected.

Look back to your answer to the third part of question 9. As you complete the next question, keep in mind those specific physical, emotional and spiritual needs that could be filled by true fellowship with other Christian women. Remember: True fellowship is more than small talk or gossip. It's about engaging in meaningful, encouraging and vulnerable conversations; giving and receiving friendly, appropriate touch; and using your gifts to serve others.

16. What specific activities might encourage the kind of fellowship that would meet those needs? (e.g., *Meet with Jan to seek advice about my marriage. Offer to clean Irene's house while she takes care of her sick child. Ask my husband to take a walk with me after work to talk about the day.*)

Here's a short list of other fellowship-building activities that you can refer back to when you need some ideas:

- Volunteer to serve in one of the areas you listed in question 11.
- Invite a friend to coffee or tea at your home or at a local café.
- Ask a friend to be your exercise partner, and then schedule a weekly time to walk, jog or ride bikes together. Be sure to plan a few minutes before or after the activity to ask the deeper questions—not while you're trying to catch your breath!
- Join a small-group Bible study.
- Make a phone date with an out-of-town friend. Send her an invi-

tation with the date and time specified so that you can both arrange to minimize distractions.

- Attend group activities at your church that reflect your age, place in life and interests, even if you don't know anyone else who will be there.

Now that you have an idea of what sort of fellowship activities you might enjoy, take a moment to work out the details. Choose one activity to schedule this week, one within a month and one before you complete this study. Complete the following information for these activities and place a check mark in the box once you have completed it.

❑ Fellowship Activity _____

    With _____ Date _____ (within one week)

    Purpose/Goal of Activity _____

❑ Fellowship Activity _____

    With _____ Date _____ (within one month)

    Purpose/Goal of Activity _____

❑ Fellowship Activity _____

    With _____ Date _____ (before completion of the study)

    Purpose/Goal of Activity _____

May your fellowship be blessed as you learn to love others with pure, Christlike love, and may you be fulfilled as you strengthen the Body of Christ with your spiritual gifts, abilities and passions.

Notes

1. This story is a fictional account. Any resemblance to actual events or people, living or dead, is purely coincidental.
2. Susie Shellenberger, *Secret Power for Girls* (Grand Rapids, MI: Zondervan Publishing House, 2003), p. 113.

EXEMPLIFYING
Goodness
STUDY

May the words of my mouth and the meditation of my heart be
pleasing in your sight, O LORD, my Rock and my Redeemer.
PSALM 19:14

We cannot learn fear of God and the basic principles of godliness, unless we are
pierced by the sword of the Spirit and destroyed. It is as if God were saying that
to rank among his sons our ordinary natures must be wiped out.
JOHN CALVIN

EVERYDAY WOMAN

"That will be $10.55."

Katie thought the clerk sounded impatient and somewhat irritated. "Tough day?" she asked. No response.

Katie opened her wallet and paused. *Hmmm*, she thought, *that doesn't seem right*. She mentally added up the prices of the items she had purchased. Noticing Katie's bewildered look, the clerk became physically agitated.

"Is there a problem, ma'am?"

For a split second Katie pictured herself replying, "No, no problem," and heading out the door. After all, it wasn't her fault the clerk was in such a hurry that she forgot to ring up the table lamp that Katie had purchased.

Maybe this was God's way of rewarding Katie for her attempt at cheering up the clerk.

"Ma'am, is there a problem?" the clerk said again, this time a little slower, enunciating each syllable.

"Oh . . . um . . . yes, actually. I think you forgot to ring up the table lamp." Katie felt her soul sigh in relief as she said the words. She knew she had done the right thing. Besides, she would have felt immense guilt every time she turned on that silly lamp if she hadn't been honest.

"Oh," the clerk mumbled, noticeably embarrassed. "Thanks for being honest. We don't see that very often around here."

The clerk smiled politely as she handed Katie her bags. *I guess I was able to brighten up her day after all,* Katie thought as she headed to her car.[1]

The Greek word for "goodness" in Galatians 5:22, *agathosune*, denotes good in the sense of what is virtuous and upright. This fruit of the Spirit not only refers to the outward appearance of good but also to the inward righteousness that penetrates the depths of a person's heart.[2] In order for the fruit of goodness to take root, our hearts must be purified and transformed by the Holy Spirit. Once our heart has been made good, the fruit we bear will necessarily follow suit. Jesus said,

> Each tree is recognized by its own fruit. People do not pick figs from thornbushes, or grapes from briers. The good man brings good things out of the good stored up in his heart, and the evil man brings evil things out of the evil stored up in his heart. For out of the overflow of his heart his mouth speaks (Luke 6:44-45).

1. How have you seen this truth manifested in the actions or words of others?

How has this truth been manifested in your own life?

Whether you feel you are bearing sweet, delicious fruit or sour grapes, the Holy Spirit wants to cultivate your heart to produce goodness in your life. To do so, He has a gardening tool He'd like you to get acquainted with—the Word of God.

ETERNAL WISDOM

C. H. Spurgeon once said of John Bunyan, "Prick him anywhere; and you will find that his blood is Bibline, the very essence of the Bible flows from him. He cannot speak without quoting a text, for his soul is full of the Word of God."[3] Wouldn't you love that to be said of you? If our very souls are filled to the brim with God's Word, nothing but sweetness can spill from our hearts, no matter how suddenly we are jarred.

Unfortunately, we can't stick a Bible under our pillows at night and transmit its contents to our sleepy little brains through osmosis. To bleed "Bibline" takes effort, determination and consistency.

2. What first comes to your mind when you hear the phrase "Bible study"?

3. How often do you *read* God's Word?

How often do you *study* His Word?

What is the difference between the two activities?

What prevents you from spending more time in God's Word?

Most of us will admit that we fall short in this area. *I can never seem to find the time. The Bible seems very confusing to me. I'm not sure where to begin.* Do any of these thoughts sound familiar? The good news is that God designed His Word to be accessible and understandable. If He wanted the message to be hidden, He wouldn't have inspired the biblical writers to record His words in human language. All the same, most of us need a little incentive and a few practical steps to get started. We'll get to the incentive later. First, let's look at three steps to get you started.

Have a Plan

Just like any good habit, the discipline of consistent Bible study takes time to develop. Have a plan of action and stick to it. Set realistic goals and build on them as you progress. Don't plan to read three chapters a day if you know you won't have time to complete them. If you start out of the gate at break-neck speeds, you will be more likely to tire and give up.

Use Study Tools

Biblical scholars have developed numerous tools to make daily reading more manageable and rewarding. The following is a list of some of these tools, as well as brief descriptions of their uses.

- **Bible Dictionary or Encyclopedia**—Similar to an English dictionary or encyclopedia, these resources give definitions and explanations of biblical terms, places and artifacts. Many include pictures and maps to help bring antiquity to life. Example: *Nelson's Illustrated Bible Dictionary.*
- **Commentary**—A commentary gives a scholar's interpretation of Bible passages. The work may be generated by one person, such as *Matthew Henry's Commentary on the Whole Bible*, or it may be a collaborative effort, such as *Robert Jamieson, A. R. Fausset and David Brown Commentary, Critical and Explanatory on the Whole Bible.*

- **Concordance**—Much like an index in the back of a book, a concordance is especially helpful for topical or word studies. This tool gives an alphabetical list of biblical themes, words or topics, coupled with corresponding verses. Most study Bibles include a small concordance or topical index, but there are entire book concordances. Examples: *Young's Analytical Concordance to the Bible; The New Strong's Exhaustive Concordance of the Bible.*
- **Devotional**—A devotional is a book comprised of short, daily readings designed to help guide a personal quiet time with God. Most devotionals are topic driven, and they usually give a key verse or passage to meditate on. Examples: *My Utmost for His Highest* by Oswald Chambers; *A Godward Life* by John Piper.
- **English Dictionary**—An English dictionary can shed new light on words we have become so accustomed to that they have lost their luster. An English dictionary is often the best place to start a word study. Example: *Merriam-Webster's Collegiate Dictionary, Eleventh Edition.*
- **Lexicon**—For those of us who never passed English in school, let alone Greek or Hebrew, a lexicon becomes a priceless tool. A lexicon generally comprises three parts: a main concordance, a dictionary of Hebrew words and a dictionary of Greek words. To use a lexicon, look up the English word in the concordance, find the corresponding Greek or Hebrew word number and then look up the number in the appropriate dictionary. Example: *The New Strong's Expanded Exhaustive Concordance of the Bible.*
- **Study Bible**—A study Bible is another excellent starting point. Choose one that includes notes, charts, maps of the Holy Land and commentary by respected Bible scholars. As you come across a verse or a passage of which you'd like a clearer understanding, simply consult the margins of the page. Examples: *The NIV Study Bible, The Ryrie Study Bible.*

Many cannot afford to have all of these books in their personal libraries. Start with a good study Bible and an English dictionary. A Bible dictionary would be a good addition. If your church has a library, you might find many of these study helps there.

Biblegateway.com [handwritten]

Learn Basic Hermeneutics   *blueletterbible.co* [handwritten]

Don't let the title scare you! Hermeneutics has been called "a million-dollar word with a bargain-basement meaning." Simply put, hermeneutics involves learning the methods for correctly interpreting the Bible.

Just like any work of literature, the Bible was written for an original audience. The biblical authors wrote in ways that the people of their time would understand. Since many years have elapsed since the writers penned their manuscripts, we have the task of figuring out what the authors intended to convey first *to their original audience* and then to us in our context.

Discern the Context

Topical study can be very beneficial, but be careful not to take verses and passages out of context. Use your study tools to help you understand the who, what, when, where, how and why of a passage. Consider the verse in light of the book, the chapter and the passage in which it appears.

4. Read Philippians 4:19. How might someone interpret this verse incorrectly by disregarding its context?

Start with the Literal

Start by assuming that a passage should be taken literally. If the passage doesn't make sense when taken at face value, then consider whether the passage falls under a different genre: metaphor, allegory, poetry, prophecy, etc. For example, Psalm 89:13 says of God, "Your arm is endued with power; your hand is strong, your right hand exalted." Since we know that God does not have physical arms or hands (see John 4:24), we can interpret this verse as an anthropomorphism—attributing human characteristics to God for literary purposes.

5. What point was the psalmist trying to make in this verse? How does the imagery used enhance the point?

Examine Cross References

Most Bibles include cross references that link a verse to other verses with similar themes or keywords that can help clarify a difficult passage. For example, Philippians 4:19 (referenced on previous page) has a cross reference to 2 Corinthians 9:8 that can further clarify the passage.

6. Read 2 Corinthians 9:8. (Don't forget the context!) What information in this verse would help you interpret Philippians 4:19 correctly?

Study History

Whether or not you enjoyed history in school, you may need to brush up on your skills as you begin studying the Bible. Correct interpretation requires learning the customs and events surrounding books of the Bible. Understanding the geography of the Holy Land is also important. Since few of us will have the opportunity to travel to Israel, take advantage of the study tools listed earlier. You'll be surprised at how vividly the pages of the Bible come alive when you understand the historical and geographical details surrounding a passage.

> **Note:** If you are interested in learning more about the topic of Bible study, we recommend reading *How to Study Your Bible* by Kay Arthur, *Personal Bible Study Methods* by Rick Warren or *How to Study the Bible* by John MacArthur.

ENDURING HOPE

As mentioned earlier, most of us need a little incentive to get us motivated enough to do so much work! Let's use the tools we've been discussing to uncover just a few of the amazing benefits we will reap as we study the Scriptures. Our text will be Psalm 19:7-11. Read these verses, and then read them in the context of the entire chapter. Look for information about the book of Psalms in your Bible. Does your Bible attribute an author to this particular psalm?

7. What did you learn about this passage by analyzing the context? (Hint: Psalm 19 is a testimony of the revelation of God. What two ways does He reveal himself to us? How does this apply to our passage?)

8. Knowing that the psalms are poetry and full of imagery, what word pictures does the psalmist use to describe God's Word and what do they teach you about His Word?

9. If your Bible includes cross-reference verses, what do they reveal about this passage?

10. David had an introspective personality. He began as a shepherd, spending much time alone in the fields with his flock. He wrote the psalms to express his thoughts. What does knowing this history reveal to you about the passage?

11. What words does David use to describe the benefits of God's Word? Look up these words using one or more of the study tools previously discussed.

12. Now it's time to apply this passage to your own life. Based on your study of Psalm 19:7-11, what benefits will you receive by studying and applying God's Word?

13. How is verse 14 linked to verses 7 to 11, and how does it apply to cultivating the fruit of goodness in your life?

When you purchase a blender, it comes with operating instructions. If you choose *not* to follow the instructions to put the lid on the container before blending a smoothie, what will happen? You'll have a huge mess! God's Word contains your operating instructions for life. You need to read and follow His instructions or risk making a huge mess of your life.

EVERYDAY LIFE

Marvin R. Vincent said that goodness "represents a stern virtue, showing itself in a zeal for truth which rebukes, corrects, and chastises, as Christ when He purged the temple."[4] Goodness is not always popular; it means choosing to be set apart from the world and to do the right thing no matter what the cost.

Take a few moments to analyze your life. Are you living righteously? Do you do the right thing, even when no one is looking? Do you feel that it's time for you to step up to the plate in regards to studying God's Word?

One of the steps we discussed earlier is to have a plan of action. Perhaps you've heard the adage "If you fail to plan, you plan to fail." That couldn't be truer of Bible study. Map out a plan for the next two weeks. Include when you'll study, what you'll study and how you plan to do it. Be realistic. If you only have 15 minutes every other day, start with that. When the two weeks are over, reevaluate. Perhaps you will be able to find *20* minutes every other day. Also decide how you will gather the tools you will need for the level of study you plan to do. You could borrow them from a friend or from a church library until you can save up the money for your own. Check secondhand bookstores or thrift shops for discounted reference books. The Internet is also a great place to find free electronic versions of some of the tools listed. Always begin your study time with prayer, asking the Holy Spirit to reveal God's Word to you (see John 14:26). If you don't already journal, now would be a good time to start by writing down what you learn each day as you study.

My Two-Week Study Plan

	Sunday	Monday	Tuesday	Wednesday	Thursday	Friday	Saturday
Time							
What I will study							
	Sunday	Monday	Tuesday	Wednesday	Thursday	Friday	Saturday
Time							
What I will study							

Tools I will need

How I will get them

Notes

1. This story is a fictional account. Any resemblance to actual events or people, living or dead, is purely coincidental.
2. James Strong, *The New Strong's Expanded Exhaustive Concordance of the Bible* (Nashville, TN: Thomas Nelson Publishers, 2001), Greek # 19.
3. C. H. Spurgeon, *Autobiography,* quoted in Iain Murray, *The Forgotten Spurgeon* (Edinburgh, Scotland: Banner of Truth Trust, 1973), p. 34, quoted in John Piper, *A Godward Life* (Sisters, OR: Multnomah Publishing, 1997), p. 17.
4. Marvin R. Vincent, "Commentary on Romans 3:12," *Vincent's Word Studies*, version 7.0.5, e-Sword.

EXPERIENCING *Peace*

SIMPLICITY AND SOLITUDE

My heart is not proud, O LORD, my eyes are not haughty; I do not concern myself
with great matters or things too wonderful for me. But I have stilled and quieted my soul;
like a weaned child with its mother, like a weaned child is my soul within me.

PSALM 131:1-2

Few people know what to do with solitude when it is forced upon them; even fewer arrange for
solitude regularly. This is not to suggest that we should neglect meeting with other believers for
prayer, but the foundation of our devotional life is our own private relationship with God.

ELISABETH ELLIOT, *ON ASKING GOD WHY*

EVERYDAY WOMAN

"Another day in paradise," Kayla mumbled as she stumbled upon a rather
large pool of water on the kitchen floor. Kayla glared at the new dishwasher.
I thought this thing was supposed to make my life easier, she grumbled to herself.
What a mess! When am I going to have time to deal with this? I'm swamped this week!

"Hey, Mom. Ugh, what happened in here?" Kayla's 14-year-old son, Caleb,
asked as he tried to dodge the puddle on his way to the table.

"Don't ask. Hey, could you grab yourself some breakfast this morning?
I'm going to be late for work. Are you coming to your sister's volleyball game
tonight?"

"Yeah, I'll be there."

"Where is Andrea, anyway? I don't hear her music blaring upstairs."

"She got a ride with her boyfriend already. See ya tonight, Mom," and he slipped out the door.

"'Bye, Caleb," she called after him, but the door had already slammed shut. *Boyfriend? When did my 17-year-old daughter get a boyfriend? This is too much. I've got to find some time to talk to her.*

Kayla slumped onto the couch while struggling to put on her high-heeled shoes. *Well, this day has gotten off to a great start, hasn't it?* she thought. She lifted her Bible from the coffee table. The thin layer of dust on the cover reminded her that the house was long overdue for some cleaning. As she turned to the Psalms, the clock caught her eye. *Why does it seem I can never find more than a few minutes, even for God?* she wondered. *When did my life get so chaotic?* She quickly scanned a few verses and then placed the Bible back on the table, being careful to match it with the dust-free rectangle. She bowed her head and quickly prayed, *Dear Lord, I'm so stressed, and it's only 7:30 a.m. Please give me Your peace today. I love You. Amen.* Kayla almost forgot her purse as she ran out the door.[1]

⸎

Do you find it ironic that despite an overabundance of time-saving, life-simplifying modern conveniences, we live frantic lives marked by stress, busyness and a lack of depth in our relationships? Can you say with the psalmist, "I have stilled and quieted my soul; like a weaned child with its mother, like a weaned child is my soul within me" (Psalm 131:2)? Like the majority of American women, your answer is probably *no.* Yet God calls us to live a life marked by His peace—a peace so pure that we can't even fully understand it (see Philippians 4:7). *surpasses all understanding* How can we attain such a magnificent peace? Before we search God's Word for the answer, take a few moments to assess your own life.

1. How would you describe peace? What qualities, actions and attitudes characterize a peaceful life?

peaceful heart + mind
free of worry + scurrying
feeling of rest-fullness

2. Based on your definitions, how would you rate the level of peace in your life on a scale of 1 to 10?

1	2	3	4	⑤	6	7	8	9	10

Peace? What's that?   Sometimes peaceful   Very peaceful

It seems nearly impossible to find peace amidst the rush of modern life, unless we escape to a quiet mountain cabin without the modern conveniences. But for most of us such an escape can only occur a few days a year—if at all! Let's discover how we can find the peace "that transcends all understanding" amidst the hurly-burly of real life. *Pergilly*

ETERNAL WISDOM

The Greek word for "peace" in Galatians 5:22 is *eirene*. This word can mean many things, including "the sense of rest and contentment" and "harmonious relationships,"[2] but in this context, scholars believe "eirene" speaks of "peace with God in a [person's] conscience"[3] and "the calm, quiet and order that takes place in a justified soul."[4]

3. According to the last two definitions of "eirene," what is the prerequisite to having true peace in your life?

   relationship with God as a believer.

   Is it possible to experience true peace apart from God? Why or why not?

   No,

4. Read Philippians 4:6-9. Once a woman has given her life to God, will she automatically experience peace? Explain.

Instead of taking steps to experience the perfect peace God offers His children, we fill our lives with things that distract us from the simple pleasures God intends for us to enjoy. In so doing, we take on a whole host of worries that really don't matter in the grand scheme of things.

5. Take a moment to reflect on your life. Place a check mark next to the items below that keep you from experiencing God's peace.

    ☑ Busyness   ☑ Unconfessed sin
    ☑ Distractions   ☑ Unhealthy relationships
    ☑ Material possessions *upkeep* ☑ Unrealistic expectations
    ☑ Money   ☐ Other:
    ☑ Noise

We'll never see the end of the distractions and worries of life unless we make a conscious effort to simplify our life and spend time in solitude with God. Only then will we be able to develop the spiritual fruit of peace.

Simplicity

What do you think of when you hear the word "simplicity"? Do you picture Laura Ingalls in *Little House on the Prairie*? A monk tending vegetables in a French monastery? Perhaps Mother Teresa or a missionary who has taken a vow of poverty? Sure we chuckle as we try to picture ourselves in one of these stereotypical roles. However, although these examples seem unrealistic in today's society, think of the measure of peace that is characterized by each of these individuals. Is that kind of peace—even a small part of it—attainable for us? It depends on how much we are willing to sacrifice to get it.

> **Simplicity (n.)** *sim-PLI-suh-t—* the state of being simple, uncomplicated or uncompounded.[5]

6. In the spaces provided, describe how each of the following categories can hinder you from developing the discipline of simplicity, and then make suggestions of how you would like to change your lifestyle to experience greater peace.

Your schedule

Your material possessions (cars, homes, appliances, etc.)

Your relationships

Your work

Your appearance

Other distractions

First Timothy 6:6 tells us that godliness with contentment, or simplicity, will result in great gain. The paradox of simplicity is that when Christ is our focus, the fewer things we have and the fewer activities we engage in, the more fulfilled we become. Getting rid of the excesses in our lives allows us to enjoy the treasures we possess.

7. According to Matthew 18:2-3, what type of heart attitude did Jesus say we must possess in order to receive the greatest treasure of all?

child like

What simple pleasures in life would this type of heart respond to?

anything

Have you ever watched a toddler open birthday presents? The child is usually so enamored with the packaging that the expensive toy within goes unnoticed. That's simplicity! It means having a heart that is easily pleased—like a child's. Choosing to walk in a park rather than watch television, arranging to visit with a friend rather than shop at the mall, or choosing a more modest lifestyle so that you can be home with your children—this is what simplicity may look like. It also means delighting in the simple truths of God's Word with renewed curiosity and interest.

8. In Psalm 131:1-2, what things did the psalmist imply would keep him from a still and quiet soul? *occupied with distractions that are complicated*

How do these things keep you from experiencing the peace of a child's heart? *distracted from simplicity*

You'll have a chance to brainstorm some practical ways to incorporate simplicity into your life a little later. But first, let's discuss another essential element of a peaceful heart.

Solitude

Whether introverted or extroverted, we each need time alone with God, away from all the distractions and constant buzz of our everyday environment: no television, no screaming kids, no music, no washing machine, no radio, no telephone and no one else—just you and God.

> We need to find God, and He cannot be found in noise and restlessness. God is the friend of silence. See how nature—trees, flowers, grass—grows in silence; see the stars, the moon and the sun, how they move in silence. . . . We need silence to be able to touch souls.—Mother Teresa[6]

9. Remember that loving others as ourselves is the second greatest commandment (see Matthew 22:37-39). How might times of solitude help us fulfill that command?

chance to really focus

10. As you read each of the following passages, note what happened before and after Jesus' times of solitude and prayer, and how those times away from the crowds affected the events that followed.

Mark 1:35-39 *early a.m. prayer, went to town to preach, cast out demons.*

Mark 6:45-51 *Feeding of 5,000 — mountains to pray — walking on water - wind ceased, disciples didnt understand - hearts were hardened.*

Mark 14:32-43 *Lords sup - Peter says he will not deny; Prayer at Gethsemane, disc sleep, prayer + sleep, Judas betrays with a kiss.*

Solitude is a vital element in our spiritual growth and in our ability to handle the circumstances we face. Finding uninterrupted time is more difficult for some of us than for others, but remember: The busier you are, the more you need times of solitude and silence for your own sanity! Be creative in finding ways to turn off the distractions. Solicit the help of family members to care for young children, or find a friend with whom you can swap day care so that each of you can recharge by spending time alone with God. If you work full-time, you may have to get up earlier or sacrifice an evening television show, but the benefits are well worth it.

ENDURING HOPE

By now you might be thinking, *It all sounds so easy on paper, but what if there's no end in sight to the commotion, busyness and complexity of life? Surely God understands that we still need to function each day, right?*

Ecclesiastes 1:9 says that there's "nothing new under the sun." We are not the first generation to struggle with finding time for God. He knows that even when our hearts desire His peace, and even though we are willing to simplify our lives and plan times of solitude with Him, there will still be some (perhaps many) times during the day when our circumstances are not conducive to peace and tranquility. However, those circumstances don't have to choke out our inner peace. In *Celebration of Discipline*, Richard Foster writes,

> There is a solitude of the heart that can be maintained at all times. Crowds, or the lack of them, have little to do with this inward attentiveness. It is quite possible to be a desert hermit and never experience solitude. . . . In the midst of noise and confusion we are settled into a deep inner silence. Whether alone or among people, we always carry a portable sanctuary of the heart.[7]

11. Based on what we've studied about simplicity and solitude, what can we do to develop this "portable sanctuary of the heart"?

How would a "deep inner silence" affect your ability to face your daily circumstances?

my resiliance would be boosted to handle the day better

12. David wrote in Psalm 23:1-3: "The Lord is my shepherd, I shall not be in want. He makes me lie down in green pastures, he leads me beside quiet waters, he restores my soul." Has there been a time in your life when you

experienced God's leading you to green pastures and quiet waters? Describe that time and how it affected you.

When we choose to spend time with God away from the fast-paced world, we will reap benefits that will sustain us during the busy, stressful times.

EVERYDAY LIFE

In this age of day planners and personal digital assistants (PDAs), it's hard to find time for anything that's not scheduled. At first, it may be necessary to schedule your times of solitude as if they were special events requiring a RSVP. Use the following invitation to schedule a rendezvous with God this week. Plan for at least a half hour and choose a place free from any distraction that might hinder your time with Him.

You're Invited, God!

Place _____

Time _____ to _____

What we'll do _____

_____

_____

While you're spending time with God, ask Him to show you practical ways that you can simplify your life so that you can enjoy inner peace amidst the turmoil of life. Write on a piece of paper or in your journal for future reference what God reveals to you. Here are a few other ideas to incorporate into this or future times of solitude:

- Choose a beautiful yet secluded location.
- Meditate on a specific verse or passage.
- Paint a picture for God.
- Read Scripture.
- Memorize a Scripture verse or two to repeat to yourself during times of stress.
- Sing praise songs or hymns.
- Write a love letter to God.
- Write in your journal.

May a simpler lifestyle, a child's heart and times of solitude bring you the peace that God desires for you, His daughter.

Notes

1. This story is a fictional account. Any resemblance to actual events or people, living or dead, is purely coincidental.
2. James Strong, *The New Strong's Expanded Exhaustive Concordance of the Bible* (Nashville, TN: Thomas Nelson Publishers, 2001), Greek #1515.
3. John Gill, "Commentary on Galatians 5:22-23," *John Gill's Exposition of the Entire Bible*, version 7.0.5, e-Sword.
4. Adam Clarke, "Commentary on Galatians 5:22-23," *Adam Clarke's Commentary on the Bible*, version 7.0.5, e-Sword.
5. *Merriam-Webster's Collegiate Dictionary*, 11th ed., s.v. "simplicity."
6. "Mother Teresa Quotes," *Brainy Quote*, 2004. http://www.brainyquote.com/quotes/quotes/m/mothert ere139219.html (accessed July 26, 2004).
7. Richard Foster, *Celebration of Discipline*, as quoted in Amy Simpson, *Diving Deep: Experiencing Jesus Through Spiritual Disciplines* (Loveland, CO: Group Publishing, 2002), p. 18.

LIVING WITH *Patience* AND *Gentleness*

SUBMISSION

If anyone wants to be first, he must be the very last, and the servant of all.

MARK 9:35

Plant patience in the garden of thy soul!
The roots are bitter, but the fruit is sweet!
And when at last it stands a tree complete,
Beneath its tender shade the burning heat
And burden of the day shall lose control—
Plant patience in the garden of thy soul!

HENRY AUSTIN DOBSON

EVERYDAY WOMAN

It was the last straw. Tori fought back tears as she walked into the living room. Her husband had carelessly thrown his coat and tie across the couch on his way to the recliner. *I just spent 15 minutes picking up after the kids,* she silently screamed. *Why can't he act like a big boy and pick up after himself?*

She knew it wasn't just her husband's negligence that was eating her. The morning's events had charted the day's course before she had time to blink. On the way to the grocery store that morning, a big truck had inched its way into her lane, causing her anger to swell. The kids in the backseat were firing questions at her the whole way.

"Mommy, can I have a snack?"

"Mommy, do frogs have fingernails?"

Tori almost asked, "Why can't you keep your questions to yourself?" but caught herself just in time. Fatigue sapped her energy, and it wasn't even lunchtime yet.

At 1 P.M., the phone rang. Tori was disappointed to find out that her mom's group—the one thing she looked forward to each week—was canceled due to the rain. *Why can't anything go my way today?* she silently moaned.

All the day's frustrations had culminated when she saw her husband's coat and tie. Tori snapped at him. He stared at her in return with eyes that clearly communicated, "What has gotten into you?" Tori knew it wasn't her finest moment, but she was so irritated, stressed and fatigued, she couldn't think clearly anymore.

"I'm sorry," Tori blurted out. "I don't know what's wrong with me, but I feel as if my whole life is on a crash course and I'm about to snap."[1]

The word "submission" has taken on a life of its own. Far from its original meaning, many women equate submission with "giving in," "weakness," "doormat" and "male-dominance." In order to understand the true meaning of submission and how it relates to the fruit of the Spirit, we must dispel any misconceptions we have about the word.

1. How would you define "submission"?

    What positive or negative connotations do you associate with the word?

    In "Becoming Like Christ," Richard Foster wrote, "Submission is the ability to lay down the everlasting burden of needing to get our own way."[2] In other words, submission is the act of setting aside or giving up our perceived rights for someone else's happiness or benefit.

2. Based on these definitions of submission, give several examples of what submission is *not*.

3. Based on Richard Foster's definition, why might submission play an important role in your relationship with God?

What might submission to God look like?

To learn more about submission and why it is so important to develop this discipline, let's take a closer look at the fruit of patience and gentleness.

ETERNAL WISDOM

In Galatians 5:22, the Greek word *macrothumia*, translated as "patience" in the *New International Version*, is "longsuffering" in the *New King James Version*. The word "long-suffering" is laden with meaning. Think about it—*long* and *suffering*. Even without knowing Greek, and without any study of the customs of the time, the implications of this term blindside us. Patience, or long-suffering, means bearing with the shortcomings of others—perhaps for long periods of time, often to our discomfort—remembering that God has put up with our shortcomings since the moment we were born.

4. According to Proverbs 19:11, what is to a person's glory?

overlooking

Col 1:13-14

In this verse, how are patience and submission related?

Many of our frustrations are born from a desire to have things our own way. Friends, coworkers, children and spouses do and say things that don't fit with the way we want things done, and we stress out. It does not matter whether our frustration is merited. By choosing to lay our desires and our way of doing things aside, we can experience peace by exercising patience, or long-suffering.

5. What people or situations tend to get under your skin?

How do you normally respond to those people or situations?

How would exercising the discipline of submission change your responses?

Just choosing to "put up with" frustrating people or situations is not enough—our attitudes must be right. That's where the fruit of gentleness comes in. The Greek word translated "gentleness" in Galatians 5:23, *praiotes*, means "meekness" or "humility."[3] In Adam Clarke's commentary, he defines "praiotes" as, "mildness; indulgence toward the weak and erring; patient suffering of injuries without feeling a spirit of revenge; an even balance of all tempers and passions; the entire opposite to anger."[4]

6. Based on these definitions, why must a spirit of gentleness accompany the fruit of patience?

How is the fruit of gentleness related to the discipline of submission?

ENDURING HOPE

Patient suffering of injuries, indulgence toward the weak, long-suffering, giving up one's rights—you may be thinking, *God doesn't really expect me to live up to these standards, does He? No human could possibly act that way, let alone have a good attitude about it!* It is a tall order, but there is hope. God never asks us to do anything that He isn't willing to empower us to do. We can do everything that God asks us to do because of Christ's power within us (see Philippians 4:13). God has also given us an example to follow.

7. According to Philippians 2:5-11, what was Jesus' position?

What did Jesus give up? What nature and sufferings did He take on?

How did Jesus' actions and attitudes exemplify the discipline of submission?

How did Jesus display the fruit of patience (long-suffering) and gentleness (humility)?

8. Restate verse 5 in your own words. How could you apply this verse to a specific situation in your life in which you need to develop the attitude of Christ?

Think like Jesus regarding everything.

Christ had every right to let us die in our sinfulness, yet He humbled Himself to the lowest point imaginable in order to save us. The concept is mind-boggling! Things that once frustrated us to no end—like someone's cutting in front of us at a busy intersection or our having to pick up after someone who is perfectly capable of doing so—are opportunities to demonstrate the attitude of Christ in us and thus obey God's command.

E V E R Y D A Y L I F E

Every woman struggles with different frustrations, depending on her personality, life stage, living situation, etc. Take a few moments to further assess what frustrations you face and how you can demonstrate patience, gentleness and submission through those circumstances.

9. Next to the following categories, record the frustrations you face in each situation.

Children

Coworkers

Driving

Friends

Parents/In-laws

Spouse

Work

Other

10. Now brainstorm specific ways that you can demonstrate patience, gentleness and submission rather than getting frustrated. Write your ideas in the spaces provided.

Children

Coworkers

Driving

Friends

Parents/In-laws

Spouse

Work

Other

11. Now think about your relationship with God. What is your attitude toward His will in your life: one of submission or rebellion?

In what areas do you need to submit your will to Him?

Spend some time in prayer. Lay your frustrations at the foot of the Cross, giving yourself and your will to God, and then rest in the assurance that the Holy Spirit will continue to cultivate the fruit of patience and gentleness as you seek to develop the discipline of submission.

Notes

1. This story is fictional. Any resemblance to actual events or people, living or dead, is coincidental.
2. Richard J. Foster, "Becoming Like Christ," *Christianity Today*, February 5, 1996, quoted at *Renovaré*, www.renovare.org/invitation_becoming_like_christ_rjf.htm (accessed August 8, 2004).
3. James Strong, *The New Strong's Expanded Exhaustive Concordance of the Bible* (Nashville, TN: Thomas Nelson Publishers, 2001), Greek #4236.
4. Adam Clarke, "Commentary on Galatians 5:22-23," *Adam Clarke's Commentary on the Bible*, version 7.0.5, e-Sword.

DISPLAYING
Kindness
SERVICE

Now that I, your Lord and Teacher, have washed your feet, you also should wash one another's feet. I have set you an example that you should do as I have done for you.

JOHN 13:14-15

Religion makes no one crabby, and morose, and sour. It sweetens the temper; corrects an irritable disposition; makes the heart kind; disposes us to make all around us as happy as possible.

ALBERT BARNES, *ALBERT BARNES' NOTES ON THE BIBLE*

EVERYDAY WOMAN

The drive to the rescue mission seemed especially long today. Haley's lower lip all but curled outward as she pouted for having to miss an aerobics class with several of her friends that evening. *I don't know why I even do this every week,* she grumbled, *maybe I should just tell them I'm too busy to volunteer anymore. No one could blame me—I've already done more than most people ever will.* Haley felt guilty as soon as she thought the words. Deep down she knew why she continued to give up her Monday evenings, and she knew that being at the mission tonight would remind her again.

As she drove, Haley thought of the faces of the regulars she would likely serve at tonight's meal: Ed, with his leathery cheeks that wrinkled when he smiled; Anna, wearing her trademark red lipstick that always ended up on her teeth; Tom, who despite being a bit grumpy, seemed to like Haley's being there every week; and a few others. Thinking about them made Haley smile. She always felt good while she was serving them—she somehow felt closer to God.

Father, she prayed silently, *change my heart before I get to the mission. Give me a renewed compassion for those I will serve tonight so that I can share Your love with them. Help me to be kind to each person—even though I don't feel like it right now—because no one else will, and because You love them just as You love me.*[1]

In the opening quote, Albert Barnes describes the essence of the fruit of kindness. Of all the people in the world, Christians have the least reason to be crabby or gloomy. God has revealed to us the secrets of a rewarding life and has filled us with His own Spirit to ensure our personal growth! With the big issues of life taken care of—why we exist, where we will spend eternity, etc.—we should be freed to be kind and polite and to spend our energy on bringing joy to others' lives through meeting their needs.

1. How does being polite and having a sweet disposition affect a Christian's witness to nonbelievers?

2. How does the fruit of kindness relate to serving others?

3. What positive and negative connotations do you associate with the word "service"?

If you equate the word "service" with being a missionary in Mozambique, you're not alone. Many are intimidated by the term because they have the impression that a life of service necessarily means taking a vow of poverty, traveling to another country or at least volunteering an infinite number of hours at a church or a local charity. While these *are* acts of service, don't become overwhelmed by thinking that your service must be on such a grand scale. Jesus showed us a different model.

ETERNAL WISDOM

Jesus exemplified a servant's heart during His three years of visible ministry. What do you picture when you think of Jesus serving others? Perhaps you see Him washing the disciples' feet in the Upper Room or dining with Simon the Leper. These examples and others give us a glimpse into Jesus' heart. While we no longer need to physically wash others' feet and we are normally not threatened by leprosy, the principles transcend our cultural differences.

4. According to Matthew 20:20-28, on what is Christ's kingdom based? What did Jesus come to do?

James and John thought Jesus was planning a physical kingdom that would overthrow the Roman rule in Israel. In essence, these two disciples were asking Jesus (it's doubtful their mother came up with the idea all on her own), "When you finally oust the Romans and become king, will you make us the grand dukes?" Jesus answered by clarifying how the royal hierarchy would work in His kingdom: "Whoever wants to become great among you must be your servant, and whoever wants to be first must be your slave" (vv. 26-27). Based on the particular words Jesus used, we could paraphrase His answer to read, "If you want to be thought of highly, you have to wait tables; and if you want to be the big boss—the head honcho, *el jefe*—then you must humble yourself and become a voluntary, willing servant."

According to His royal hierarchy, Jesus would be (and is) the King because He gave up His life to become the ultimate servant. As his subjects, we can please the King by waiting on tables or serving those around us.

This paradox may be familiar to you, but do you live it daily? Reflect on your life as we explore three principles of service.

Serve Those Within Your Realm

According to the Gospel accounts of Christ's miracles, Jesus rarely—if ever—sought out people to heal. He ministered to those who came to Him: the paralyzed man who was dropped through the roof (see Mark 2:3-5), the two blind men who shouted at Him from the side of the road (see Matthew 20:29-34), the woman who touched His cloak as He walked (see Mark 5:25-34), and the list goes on.

5. What does Jesus' model of healing teach you about service?

6. Give several examples of people whom God placed within your realm as an opportunity to serve this past week. Include family members, friends, coworkers or anyone that you feel could have used your kindness or had needs that you could have met.

Did you take the opportunity to serve those He put before you? How might you better serve these people in the future?

Serve Those Outside Your Realm

God has a special place in His heart for the poor, the oppressed, the sick and the unlovable; as His representatives, so should we. As the Holy Spirit develops the fruit of kindness in our hearts, compassion, mercy and justice will follow.

7. As you read the following verses, write what each verse teaches us about mercy, justice, compassion and service.

Hosea 6:6 *heart vs Ritual*

Micah 6:8 *He gave an example of justice humility, love Kindness*

Luke 10:27 *all heart, soul + mind + neighbor as yourself.*

Galatians 5:13 *we are free to serve others.*

James 1:22,27 *do it! Visit orphans + widows*

James 2:14-17

God called Mother Teresa to a life of what some would call *extreme* service, but though she spent each day serving the poorest of the poor in India and other countries, Mother Teresa understood that Christ's call to serve the poor was not limited to the physically impoverished.

> The suffering [in Calcutta] is much more physical, much more material, but in some other places . . . suffering is much deeper and also it's more hidden. You can find Calcutta all over the world if you have eyes to see; not only to *see* but to *look*. . . . Material poverty you can always satisfy with material. The unwanted, the unloved, the uncared [for], the forgotten, the lonely—this is much greater poverty. —Mother Teresa (emphasis added)[2]

8. What hidden suffering do you see among the people of our nation? Within your community?

9. What is the difference between eyes that *see* suffering people and eyes that *look* for them?

Which type of eyes do you have? Explain.

Serve with Pure Motives

Jesus criticized the religious leaders of His day for being hypocrites—for showing outward piety while their hearts were not right with God. Though we perform great acts of service, if our motives are impure, our efforts are in vain. Sure, we may relieve someone's physical suffering or help someone feel loved, but ultimately our acts will not please God.

10. Read Matthew 25:31-46. What does the response of the righteous in verses 37 and 38 indicate about their motives for serving the hungry, the thirsty, the sick, etc.?

If these people's motives were not to get into heaven and they did not realize that their acts of service were to Christ Himself, what do you think motivated these people to take care of those in need?

When you serve others, what motivates you?

If your motivation to serve is a desire to gain others' approval, to assuage a guilty conscience or to make an effort to be good enough to enter heaven, ask God to transform your heart. Ask Him to bring you to a place where you can say, like Mother Teresa,

> I do it for Jesus. He is my all. If He is my all, then I must be able to talk to people of the person I love. Because I love Him I am here today. I do it for Jesus, for the greater glory of God and the good of people.[3]

ENDURING HOPE

One of the great paradoxes of the discipline of service is that when we put others before ourselves, we find the greatest fulfillment. Haley, our Everyday Woman, learned this principle in an indirect way. Even though she didn't *feel* like serving the homeless that night, she knew that once she got to the mission and began interacting with those she was serving, her heart would change and she would be glad she went.

11. Describe a time when you didn't feel like serving someone but did it anyway. How did you feel afterward? How did that experience affect your attitude toward serving that person in the future?

There is great hope in knowing that when we obey God by putting others before ourselves—even when we don't feel like it—He will bless us with joy as we serve.

12. Review Matthew 25:34-40. What other blessings will we receive as a result of serving others?

We find another source of hope in realizing that we don't have to do it all. Service is not about how much we do or how big our acts of service are. Christ honored the righteous for giving a simple glass of water to a thirsty person (see Matthew 25:35). Supplying snacks for Vacation Bible School or a Sunday School class can be an honorable act of service!

13. In John 6:5-14, how did God bless many through one young boy's sacrificial act?

What does this story tell you about God's ability to use you?

Our job is to put others before ourselves. God can take our feeble efforts and turn them into great acts of service.

EVERYDAY LIFE

God is so creative! We can see His ingenuity in creation, in His Word and through Jesus' example on Earth. Genesis 1:26 says that God made humankind according to His likeness, which explains why we also have a propensity for creativity.

Choose one (or both) of the options below; however, don't confine yourself to these parameters. Allow yourself the freedom to expand on or modify these exercises to suit your personality and creativity.

Words Full of Art

For this activity, you will need an 8½x11-inch (or larger) piece of paper, card stock or poster board, and colored felt-tip pens, pencils or paints. Based on all you have learned in this session about service and kindness, create a word and/or picture collage. For example, you could draw pictures of you serving someone God has put in your path—such as your spouse or a difficult coworker—and then act it out during the week. Or you could write keywords or phrases that describe a heart of service, such as "kind," "humble," "patient," etc.

Words from the Heart

For this activity you will need a piece of stationery and a pen. Write a letter to God expressing your desire to serve Him by serving others. Thank Him for the things He has already taught you and ask Him to give you eyes that not only *see* suffering but eyes that *look* for the lonely, the abandoned, the hungry, the thirsty so that you can minister to those people. Be honest about your fears and your expectations.

> **Note:** If you are doing this study with a group of women, bring your "Words Full of Art" or "Words from the Heart" activity to your next group meeting.

Notes

1. This story is fictional. Any resemblance to actual events or people, living or dead, is coincidental.
2. Ann Petrie and Jeanette Petrie, *Mother Teresa: The Legacy*, VHS (Canada: Petrie Productions, 2003).
3. Ibid.

WALKING IN
Faithfulness
INTEGRITY

In my integrity you uphold me and set me in your presence forever.

PSALM 41:12

Let my name stand among those who are willing to bear ridicule and reproach
for the truth's sake, and so earn some right to rejoice when the victory is won.

LOUISA MAY ALCOTT, IN A LETTER TO LUCY STONE

EVERYDAY WOMAN

Kailey stubbed her little toe as she hopped over toys and her six-month-old on the way to the telephone. She grimaced but managed to hold in a yelp as she picked up the receiver.

"Hello?" she said, as evenly as possible.

"Hi, Kailey, this is Sarah. My small group just had someone cancel for our trip to the water park on Thursday, and I was hoping you'd like to go. The ticket's already paid for and everything."

"How fun!" Kailey exclaimed. "I would love to." But as soon as she said the words, Kailey remembered that she had already made plans for Thursday to visit her younger sister, Jenny, while she was home from college. Kailey's heart sank. How often did she get a chance to go do fun things with women her age? And a free ticket to a water park seemed too good to be true, since money had been tight lately. *I'm sure Jenny would understand*, Kailey thought. *She probably has other friends she could visit that day anyway. But I did tell her I would be home, and she* is *my sister. I would feel awful if she ditched me for last-minute plans.*

"Great!" Sarah replied. "Do you want me to pick you up on my way?"

Kailey felt warm and noticed a lump growing in her throat. She swallowed hard and said, "Actually, Sarah, I just remembered that my sister is going to be in town that day and I already made plans to hang out with her. I really appreciate you thinking of me, though."

When Kailey hung up the phone, she felt disappointed, but mostly relieved. She knew that being a woman of her word was more important—and more rewarding—than a day at a water park.[1]

Although faith in God is a vital part of spiritual growth, the spiritual fruit of faithfulness (the Greek word *pistis*) is best understood as fidelity or trustworthiness rather than a spiritual trust in the unseen. Faithfulness means keeping your word, taking care of those things entrusted to you, being fair, punctual, honest and just.

1. Look up the word "integrity" in a dictionary. What correlation do you see between integrity and the characteristics of faithfulness?

   adherence to moral principles

2. Describe a time when you had a similar experience in which your integrity or faithfulness was challenged. What were the results of your choice?

In session 2 we learned that in order to demonstrate the fruit of goodness, our hearts must be transformed by God's Word and His Holy Spirit. Once a person's heart is made good, the fruit it produces will be sweet and beneficial (see Luke 6:43-45). The same is true of the fruit of faithfulness and the discipline of integrity—they each spring from a heart that seeks God and desires to grow spiritually. The difference between the spiritual fruits of goodness and faithfulness is that the former emphasizes beneficence—kindness and charity—while the latter emphasizes moral integrity and trustworthiness.

By definition, "integrity" is a "firm adherence to a code of especially moral values."[2] As Christians, our code of moral values comes from the principles set forth by God and communicated to us through the Bible. There are many characteristics of integrity, including loyalty to one's spouse and children, responding to duty and accepting responsibility, but in the interest of time, let's briefly explore the following five essentials to a life of integrity.

Pursue Truth

Truth is what is right and pure and good. Pursuing truth is a lifelong journey. This characteristic of integrity means that we will not only _choose_ truth when we are faced with right and wrong, but that we will _seek_ it.

3.   What does Jesus' statement in John 14:6 teach you about the nature of truth?

Based on this verse, how might you pursue truth?

4. According to John 16:13-14, who is responsible for guiding you into truth? *Holy Spirit*

   Where does He learn this truth? *Father*

5. Based on what you have learned from these verses and on your personal experience, give some specific examples of how you can pursue, or seek out, truth.

Be Honest

Telling the truth sounds simple enough, doesn't it? It's one of those things we assume we all learn as children, and we pat ourselves on the back because we don't tell "big" lies. But upon closer examination, are we always truthful? Do we always do what we say we will? Do we ever exaggerate—just a little—to make a story more interesting? Do we ever back ourselves into a corner until we're confined by our own lies?

6. What do the following verses teach us about honesty? How could you apply these verses to your own life?

   Deuteronomy 25:15-16

   Proverbs 11:1; 20:23

   Proverbs 24:26

   Luke 16:10

God hates dishonesty. A woman of integrity guards her lips from speaking anything that isn't true, and she lovingly confronts others when they are untruthful.

Being a woman of your word falls under this moral principle. James 5:12 says, "Let your 'Yes' be yes, and your 'No,' no." When you say you will do something, do it! If you tell someone that you will call that evening, make the time to do it. At the very least, make it a point to call and say that you're busy, but will call back the next day. Whether the person will mind if you don't call is not the point—common courtesy and moral integrity is.

Love Justice and Mercy

Christianity itself is based on God's infinite justice and unfathomable mercy. Were God solely just, we would all be sent to hell on account of our sin. But because He is also full of mercy, He saves from eternal punishment those who choose to repent and follow Him.

7. According to Zechariah 7:9, what three things are we instructed to do?

   mercy
   justice
   compassion

8. Now read Micah 6:8. What does humility have to do with justice and mercy?

   do justice
   love kindness
   walk humbly ō God

Jesus criticized the Pharisees because they went so far as to tithe 10 percent of their garden herbs, yet neglected the "weightier matters of the law": justice, mercy and faithfulness (see Matthew 23:23). Notice that Jesus did not say that they were wrong to perform spiritual duties such as tithing but only that they should not have neglected the more important things.

9. Consider Matthew 23:23. In what way might we perform spiritual

duties while neglecting the more important values of our Christian faith?

How have you experienced this in your own life?

Show Concern for Others

The command to love others as ourselves is only second to loving the God of the universe (see Matthew 22:39). How we treat others shows whether God's love is within us.

10. Romans 12:9-21 is full of instructions for interpersonal relationships. Read the passage, noting the commands related to your treatment of others. List those commands that are especially difficult for you to follow.

11. How might the principles found in Philippians 2:3-4 help you work on the commands you listed in question 10?

Having a genuine concern for others will affect the way you speak to them, listen to them, act toward them and respond to them. It will also cause you to respect their property. When you borrow something, instead of allowing it to disappear in a closet for months, return it in a timely manner. These seemingly small things demonstrate integrity.

Develop a Strong Work Ethic

A strong work ethic is important whether you are a stay-at-home mom or a woman in the workplace. Both are opportunities to labor as "for the Lord, and not for men" (Colossians 3:23). Ecclesiastes 9:10 says, "Whatever your hand finds to do, do it with all your might."

12. In what ways might an employee show a strong work ethic in the workplace?

13. In what ways might a stay-at-home mom demonstrate a strong work ethic to her family and others?

14. How might displaying a strong work ethic—either in the home or in the workplace—act as a witness of your faith?

Integrity is best tested in the little things and in the times when we are alone. Recall the words of Luke 16:10, "Whoever can be trusted with very little can also be trusted with much, and whoever is dishonest with very little will also be dishonest with much." Ask God to help you be faithful in the small—and large—situations you face each day.

ENDURING HOPE

Developing the discipline of integrity simply because we're commanded to would be reason enough. Knowing that the way we live our lives directly affects the way others view God would also be enough. But because of God's grace, He abundantly blesses us for our obedience. If for no other reason, live a faithful life because *the benefits are worth it!* Let's look at just a few of those benefits together.

15. What are the benefits of living a life of integrity according to each of the following verses?

Psalm 25:21

Psalm 41:12

Proverbs 10:9

Proverbs 11:3

God loves when His children choose obedience. He loves it so much that He is willing to *bless* us for what we're already *supposed to* do! Take a few moments to thank God for protecting, guiding, upholding, securing and placing in His presence those children who walk uprightly. Then ask Him to continue to develop the fruit of faithfulness and the discipline of integrity in your life.

Have you ever read a choose-your-own-adventure book in which you make choices that affect the outcome of the story? The following exercise is similar; however, instead of simply choosing the outcome of the story, you are going to write it.

Read each of the following scenarios. In the space provided, finish the story. You can decide whether the person will choose to do right or wrong, but be sure to include the consequences of either decision.

> **Scenario A**—Julie opened a package on her front porch to find a duplicate of a Christian book she ordered. Even though she already received the one she paid for, she knows of another woman who could really use this one.

> **Scenario B**—Tanya stumbles into work 15 minutes late, but when she tries to let her boss know she'll work extra to make it up, he isn't in yet.

> **Scenario C**—Nicole is relieved when Amber finally comes to pick up her kids. Nicole didn't mind watching them once or twice, but she's had enough. Before leaving, Amber asks, "Nicole, would you mind watching them again next Tuesday for a couple of hours?"

Notes

1. This story is fictional. Any resemblance to actual events or people, living or dead, is coincidental.
2. *Merriam-Webster's Collegiate Dictionary*, 11th ed., s.v. "integrity."

Practicing
SELF-CONTROL
FASTING

Jesus declared, "I am the bread of life. He who comes to me will never go hungry, and he who believes in me will never be thirsty."

JOHN 6:35

What a curious phenomenon it is that you can get men to die for the liberty of the world who will not make the little sacrifice that is needed to free themselves from their own individual bondage.

BRUCE BARTON

E V E R Y D A Y W O M A N

Chloe held the spiral-bound journal delicately, carefully turning the pretty floral pages. It was a priceless treasure—the thoughts, feelings, prayers and whimsical dreams of a very difficult year of her life. She liked to pull it out every so often to relive the lessons learned that year. A knowing smile danced on her lips as she came across a very familiar group of entries.

> *August 4th—Still don't know what to do about the job in Houston. Have been convicted that I should fast until Friday, when I must give my decision. I'm scared to death—three days without food!—but confident that God will give me strength.*

August 5th—My stomach hates me, but I feel a peace that I cannot explain. Praying during my usual mealtimes has been a precious escape.

August 6th—Someone is barbequing, and I wish my sense of smell wasn't so keen. Although I still don't know what I should tell my boss tomorrow, I am overwhelmed by a sense that whatever I choose, God will go before me.

August 7th—I decided to take the job. Looking back, I can see that although my fasting did not invoke divine revelation, it was never meant to. God simply wanted to get my heart in a place where I could feel His peace. I'm so thankful for the past three days. And now it's time to get some grub![1]

Modern America mirrors the great Roman Empire in many ways—our power, our prestige and our insatiable appetite for sensual pleasure (aka hedonism). Just look around you. How many restaurants and fast-food eateries can you name, just in your town? How many TV shows, movies and sporting events do you have access to at any given moment? How easy is it to obtain sexually immoral material? Our affluence and declining morals have placed countless pleasures at our fingertips.

1. What are examples of our society being obsessed with seeking pleasure?

2. How might pleasures—even those that God originally created for our enjoyment—become idols in our lives?

"Sexual immorality," "gluttony," "debauchery"—these are no longer words reserved for an ancient civilization—they define the world around us. Solomon declared in Ecclesiastes 1:9-10, "there is nothing new under the sun," and the writers of the New Testament observed firsthand many people in their culture who were intent on constant pleasure. Clearly, the warnings they gave to men and women 2,000 years ago apply to us today.

ETERNAL WISDOM

The spiritual fruit of self-control is the Christian's weapon against excessive pleasures that can divert our passion from God to earthly things. The Greek word for "self-control" in Galatians 5:23, *egkrateia*, is "the virtue of one who masters [her] desires and passions, especially [her] sensual appetitites."[2] Adam Clarke defines this fruit as "a proper and limited use of all earthly enjoyments, keeping every sense under proper restraints, and never permitting the animal part to subjugate the rational."[3]

3. How might a limited use of the pleasures that God created for our enjoyment—such as food and entertainment—benefit us?

God's amazing gifts to His children include the ability to taste, touch, smell, see and hear. A juicy summer-ripened peach, a warm embrace, the invigorating smell of salt and seaweed at the beach, a picture-perfect sunset, the sounds produced by a master pianist—we could enjoy none of these pleasures without our senses. God delights to pleasure us with His creation. However, as with many of the good gifts that God has given us, we can allow sensual pleasures to take the place of God in our lives.

4. A sensual appetite is an inherent craving to satisfy one or more of our five senses. How would you describe a woman who has mastered her sensual appetites? What would she act like? Look like? How would she feel about herself? About God?

5. Self-control (egkrateia) comes from the Greek word *kratos*, meaning "strength."[4] What role does strength play in restraining us from satisfying every craving we have for pleasure?

Whose strength must we ultimately rely on? Why?

Fasting

Craving food—as well as any obsession associated with it, such as chronic dieting, anorexia, bulimia, obesity, excessive preoccupation with food, gluttony—is a sensual appetite that we must master. We are a craving-driven society, which has catapulted many women into a vicious cycle. Our hedonistic eating patterns have caused a frightening rise in obesity. This trend has in turn caused a backlash of eating disorders among women who constantly compare themselves with fashion models. Our misconstrued ideas of how much food our body needs to function properly leads to overeating and obesity, and the cycle continues.

Note: Fasting should be entered into prayerfully, making sure your purpose is clear. Consult a physician before determining how long a fast should be or whether it is appropriate, especially if you are pregnant, breast feeding, or have diabetes, hypoglycemia, an eating disorder or any other physical condition that might make fasting harmful to your health.

If you are suffering from an eating disorder such as anorexia, bulimia, chronic dieting or obesity, we advise you to seek help from a reputable Christian nutritionist and/or counselor. Your pastor or doctor may be able to guide you in finding the right person, or you can call Focus on the Family's counseling department (1-800-A-Family or 1-719-531-3400) for a free consultation by a licensed counselor[5] and

Our society's preoccupation with image and pleasure seeking has caused us to disregard a very important spiritual discipline: fasting. While fasting has some positive physical effects, the biblical reasons for fasting were primarily spiritual. For the purpose of this study, we'll focus on fasting in a spiritual context.

6. Describe your experience(s) with fasting. If you have never fasted, describe your feelings about this discipline.

7. Read the following statements about fasting. Place a check mark next to each statement with which you agree.

   ❏ Fasting is dangerous to my health.
   ❏ Fasting will make me too tired to function during the day.
   ❏ Fasting will send my body into starvation mode, causing it to consume healthy muscle fibers and body tissues.
   ❏ Fasting is legalistic.
   ❏ I've never given much thought to fasting.
   ❏ Since the Bible does not contain any "thou shalt fast" commands, it is irrelevant today.

8. According to Matthew 9:14-15, why didn't Jesus' disciples fast?

   When did Jesus imply they would fast?

   What does this imply about whether we should fast?

In *Celebration of Discipline*, Richard Foster writes,

> In the coming of Jesus, a new day had dawned. The kingdom of God had come among them in present power. The Bridegroom was in their midst; it was a time for feasting, not fasting. There would, however, come a time for His disciples to fast, although not in the legalism of the old order. . . . It is clear from this passage that Christ both upheld the discipline of fasting and that He anticipated that His followers would do it.[6]

The Jews had days of fasting to remind themselves of national disasters (see Zechariah 8:19); for the annual day of atonement, Yom Kippur (see Leviticus 16:29,31); for mourning after the death of a loved one (see 1 Samuel 31:13); for penance before God (see 1 Kings 21:27); for special favors from God (see 2 Samuel 12:16); for direction (see Ezra 8:23); for when they were in deep trouble (see 1 Samuel 7:6); and for loosing the bonds of oppression (see Isaiah 58:3-9). Some rabbis recommended fasting on Mondays and Thursdays. However, because Jesus did not command us to fast at specified times, we are free to exercise this discipline as we feel led by the Spirit.

9. Describe some appropriate and/or beneficial times to fast. Remember, biblical fasting always centers on spiritual purposes.

Three types of fasts are mentioned in the Bible: the basic fast, the partial fast and the supernatural fast.

> **Basic Fast**—Refraining from all food and beverages for one or more days, drinking only water (see Esther 4:16). **Note:** If you have never fasted before, it is suggested that you consult with your physician before fasting for more than three days.
> **Partial Fast**—Choosing to abstain from certain foods and/or beverages for a length of time (see Daniel 10:3).
> **Supernatural Fast**—Going without food or water for a supernat-

ural length of time (see Deuteronomy 9:9; 1 Kings 19:8). **Note:** We do not recommend this type of fast.

For more information on the topic of fasting, including reasons to fast and practical tips on fasting, we recommend *The Beginner's Guide to Fasting* by Elmer Towns (Regal Books, 2001).

Whether you abstain from one meal or fast for many days, remember that—as with all things—God is most concerned about your heart attitude.

10. What did Jesus condemn in Matthew 6:16-18? What did He condone?

What benefit will we receive if we fast for God's eyes only and not to gain others' respect or approval?

Abstaining from Other Hindrances

If the purpose of fasting is to avoid being controlled by an otherwise beneficial pleasure, we could feasibly apply this discipline to other areas of our lives. We can abstain from just about anything that distracts us from the true source of our fulfillment. As we voluntarily give up something we desire for a time, we are free to focus our desire where it belongs.

11. What pleasures or distractions other than food might hinder you from devoting your passion, time and energy to God and His purposes for your life? Be specific.

newspaper
TV
cozy quiet evening

In his book *Walking with Saints*, Calvin Miller writes,

> This is our culture of convenience. We are the well-fed, the secure. We are lovers of the large plate and the broad sofa. Material abundance keeps us from seeking any other kind. But could it be that our wonderful, abundant culture is really the jackal that preys on our peace?[7]

12. How might abstaining from the sensual pleasures you listed in question 11 free you to seek spiritual abundance and experience true fulfillment and peace?

ENDURING HOPE

One of the great paradoxes of the Christian life is that in exercising discipline we find the greatest freedom. In choosing to bring our bodies under submission—including our desires for food, entertainment and physical gratification—we experience the greatest pleasure.

Paul gives us a picture of another reward of self-control in 1 Corinthians 9:24-27. Read these verses, and then answer the following questions:

13. To what race did Paul refer in these verses? For what crown are we competing?

14. What did Paul say would disqualify him from the race?

Who else would be affected if Paul were disqualified from the race?

In verse 25, Paul says that whoever plans to compete in the competition must go into "strict training." This phrase is the Greek word *egkrateuomai*.[8] Does that sound familiar? It is very similar to the word for self-control that we studied earlier. Let's paraphrase Paul's analogy using a modern-day sporting event: the Olympics.

In the Olympics, only the very best win the gold. Olympians exercise tremendous self-control to get their bodies in shape for competition, competing for a little piece of metal and the promise of fleeting fame and money. How much more should we practice self-control since we're competing for a much more significant prize? The fans who watch the Olympics are like those we have told about God. They are watching our every move! That's why self-control is so important. If we don't keep our physical desires under control, we will not only forfeit the reward, but we'll discredit our Christian witness.

15. Have you ever watched a Christian bring shame to God because of a lack of self-control? Explain.

16. How could exercising self-control positively affect your Christian witness?

Review your answers to question 11 again. Also consider whether food has become an idol in your life, stealing the devotion that belongs to Christ alone. Spend a few minutes in prayer, asking God to reveal any areas of your life where you lack self-control. Then ask Him to impress on your heart the specific actions you need to take to break the hold that seeking pleasure has on your life. When you are finished praying, record your thoughts in the space provided. Also record your thoughts, feelings and progress as you put into practice the disciplines that God has laid on your heart.

Dec 12ᵗʰ   12-12-12

Notes

1. This story is a fictional account. Any resemblance to actual events or people, living or dead, is coincidental.

2. James Strong, *The New Strong's Expanded Exhaustive Concordance of the Bible* (Nashville, TN: Thomas Nelson Publishers, 2001), Greek #1466.

3. Adam Clarke, "Commentary on 2 Peter 1:6," *Adam Clarke's Commentary on the Bible*, version 7.0.5, e-Sword.

4. Strong, *The New Strong's Expanded Exhaustive Concordance of the Bible*, Greek #1466.

5. Counselors at Focus on the Family are licensed in the state of Colorado.

6. Richard Foster, *Celebration of Discipline*, 3rd ed. (New York: Harper Collins, 1998), pp. 46-47.

7. Calvin Miller, *Walking with Saints*, quoted in Amy Simpson, *Diving Deep: Experiencing Jesus Through Spiritual Disciplines* (Loveland, CO: Group Publishing, 2002), p. 33.

8. Strong, *The New Strong's Expanded Exhaustive Concordance of the Bible*, Greek #1467.

CULTIVATING *Joy*

CELEBRATION

Rejoice in the Lord and be glad, you righteous; sing, all you who are upright in heart!

PSALM 32:11

People who want to pursue joy especially need to practice the discipline of celebration. This is a primary reason that we see much emphasis placed on feast days in the Old Testament. Times of feasting were to be transforming experiences—just as times of meditation or fasting were.

JOHN ORTBERG, *THE LIFE YOU'VE ALWAYS WANTED*

EVERYDAY WOMAN

Rachel glanced at her watch. The dial read 10:32 A.M. *When is this sermon going to end?* she thought, while flipping idly through the pages of her Bible. She felt bad about not paying attention, but she just wasn't in the mood to be preached at. She wasn't in the mood for much these days, except thinking about how miserable she was since Rick broke up with her. She felt depressed and lonely, and nothing seemed to cheer her up. She had tried going shopping with her friends, but that just made her wish she had the money to buy that adorable pair of chinos. She tried burning all his letters, but she ended up crying for an hour and a half. She even tried hot fudge sundaes—nothing seemed to bring a smile to her face.

Rachel turned the pages of her Bible gingerly, trying to avoid a disapproving look from the woman next to her. Rachel paused when she saw Psalm 100: "Shout for joy to the LORD . . . come before him with joyful songs. . . . Enter his gates with thanksgiving . . . give thanks to him and praise his name." Rachel felt awful. She hadn't done any of those things since her dreams were shattered two months ago. She wondered if secretly she blamed God for letting Rick leave. She read the last two lines of the psalm again: "For the LORD is good and his love endures forever; his faithfulness continues through all generations." Suddenly Rachel knew why she had been miserable. It wasn't because God wasn't faithful to her; it was because she had been so preoccupied with herself.

O Lord, Rachel silently prayed, *forgive me for not thanking You in all things. You really have taken such good care of me these past two months. And maybe You have a reason for taking Rick away, maybe you have something better in store for me—I don't know. But I do know that I can trust You because You love me. So even though I don't feel like shouting for joy right now, help me to have a thankful heart and worship You nonetheless.*[1]

God has given us many reasons to celebrate! Why do many of us live as if we're trying not to laugh? We women are notorious for letting the pressures of life, others' expectations and the mundane activities of daily living squelch the immense joy that the Holy Spirit desires to cultivate in us.

1. On a scale of 1 to 10, how would you rate the amount of joy and laughter in your life?

1	2	3	4	5	6	7	8	9	10

What's joy?   Laugh occasionally   Always joyful

2. Why do you think women have such a difficult time just being happy?

What circumstances and attitudes hinder our enjoyment of life?

3. What circumstances, events or attitudes hinder you from experiencing the joy of the Lord?

Imagine how much more enjoyable life would be if we would remember to laugh at life's little mishaps, if we would find reasons to smile amidst the ordinary duties of the day and if we would be thankful and rejoice in all the little blessings God provides to season our lives with pleasure. Let's look more closely at the spiritual fruit of joy and its cousin, the discipline of celebration.

ETERNAL WISDOM

The Greek word translated "joy" in Galatians 5:22, *chara*, is akin to *chairo*, meaning "to rejoice."[2] The English word "joy" is from a Latin word also meaning "to rejoice."[3] There is a correlation between the feelings of joy and happiness we experience and our decision to actively rejoice and be thankful for the things with which God blesses us. We have a direct influence on our level of joy based on whether we choose to rejoice in all things.

4. According to the following verses, for what things does a Christian have reason to rejoice?

Matthew 7:11

Romans 8:28

1 Corinthians 1:26-30

Col. 3:1-4 Keep Seeking –

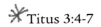 Titus 3:4-7

Hebrews 2:11

What other things can you think of for which a Christian can rejoice?

Philippians 4:4 says, "Rejoice in the Lord always. I will say it again: Rejoice!" Notice that this verse does not command us to rejoice in our circumstances, in our accomplishments or in our affluence.

5. Why would Paul tell us to rejoice in the Lord rather than in these things?

The basis of a Christian's joy is knowing that we have been saved from death, have been pardoned by the God of the universe and can now enjoy a *personal* relationship with Him. We have the ultimate reason to celebrate: We can live life with a clear conscience and in the power of the Holy Spirit! And we can be free from anxiety and care, even amidst difficult circumstances.

6. How is this Christian joy different from the world's definition of happiness?

How are happiness and joy linked? Can you have one without the other? Explain?

7. How is joy linked with the spiritual disciplines we have been studying?

According to Richard Foster, "Celebration is central to all the Spiritual Disciplines. Without a joyful spirit of festivity the Disciplines become dull, death-breathing tools in the hands of modern Pharisees."[4]

8. Do you agree with this statement? Explain.

What verses support your answer?

9. How might you incorporate a "joyful spirit of festivity" into each of the following disciplines? Be as specific as possible.

Fellowship

Study

Simplicity

Solitude

Submission

Service

Integrity

Fasting

The discipline of celebration is the physical manifestation of a heart of joy. God wants us to experience the refreshing fun of celebration to temper the inevitable times of sadness and mourning.

The feasts of the Old Testament were festivals commanded by God to commemorate the great spiritual events of Israel's history: Passover, the Feast of Weeks, the Feast of Tabernacles, the Feast of Ingathering, the Sabbath, the Feast of Unleavened Bread.[5] Each was an opportunity to corporately commemorate the amazing things that God had done and would continue to do in their lives.

10. What feasts could we celebrate as the Body of Christ? As families? As individuals?

Obviously not all celebration must (or should) revolve around food. What alternative ways can you think of to celebrate?

Consider the following quote:

Out of our broken lives God brings forth the fruit of his kingdom. Can you see it in your life? From your branches hang sweet fruit—

love, peace, patience, gentleness, and self-control. Lessons learned. Changes made. Relationships healed. Hope restored. It is all *his* doing. That's why we mark it with celebration (emphasis in original).[6]

11. How do these words personally relate to the journey you've taken through the past seven sessions?

How might you celebrate—or commemorate in the future—the growth you've experienced through this study?

Remember that spiritual disciplines require work on our part. Practicing celebration requires planning and energy, but the rewards are well worth the effort.

ENDURING HOPE

Paul understood that he could place no confidence in his earthly flesh, but that once he was resurrected from the dead like his Lord, Jesus Christ, then he could *truly* celebrate. He encouraged the Philippians to embrace this thinking.

12. According to Philippians 3:12-21, what prize did Paul strain to obtain?

13. Paul said that we should "live up to what we have already attained" (v. 16). What did he mean by this statement?

How do his words relate to the growth you have experienced through this study?

14. For what do Christians eagerly await?

One of the greatest sources of hope—and joy—in a believer's life should be the realization that one day we will be perfected. One day we will say sayonara to our sinful flesh and unruly hearts and be able to worship God in complete purity and peace. On that day, we will kiss the struggles of spiritual disciplines good-bye, because in our perfected state we will be completely loving, joyful, peaceful, patient, kind, good, faithful, gentle and self-controlled. That's a reason to celebrate!

EVERYDAY LIFE

This side of heaven, we still have many reasons to celebrate. We've already discussed many of them, but let's think of some more.

15. Brainstorm reasons you have to celebrate—both big and small (e.g., God's creation, a birth, a baptism, the birth, death and resurrection of our Savior).

Earlier, we learned that the Old Testament feasts were instituted to commemorate events that had happened in the past. Remembering the good gifts and victories God had given the Israelites gave them hope for the future. When faced with trying circumstances, remembering God's faithfulness in the past renewed their devotion to Him.

A Book of Celebration is a great way to chronicle the blessings, events and triumphs of life to look back on when things get difficult. Your book could take a number of forms. Choose a type of book from the list below or think of your own way to record God's faithfulness. Begin today!

Book of Celebration Ideas

- Fill a three-ring binder with several pieces of colored construction paper. Title each page with a reason to celebrate, such as "creation," "family," etc. Then over the months fill in the pages with words, pictures, stickers—anything that reminds you of the blessings in your life.
- If you like to create scrapbooks, create one specifically for the *spiritual* milestones in your and your loved ones' lives. Include pictures and memorabilia from baptisms, commitments to Christ, meaningful retreats, etc.
- If you love to write, a prayer journal can be transformed into a Book of Celebration simply by focusing on the positive blessings and answered prayer in your life rather than the negative issues you face. Or create a separate journal specifically to record reasons for joy and celebration, as well as your thoughts and feelings surrounding spiritual milestones.
- Invite family members to help create the memorable pages so that they can take ownership of the times of celebration and reap the benefits of joy.

Note: If you're completing this study with a group of women, bring your Book of Celebration—however much you have completed—to your next group meeting.

May your life be marked by joy and celebration as you continue to grow more into the likeness of our Savior, Jesus Christ, and may you be blessed as you practice spiritual disciplines and allow the Holy Spirit to cultivate His fruit within you.

Notes

1. This story is fictional. Any resemblance to actual events or people, living or dead, is coincidental.
2. James Strong, *The New Strong's Expanded Exhaustive Concordance of the Bible* (Nashville, TN: Thomas Nelson Publishers, 2001), Greek #5479.
3. *Merriam-Webster's Collegiate Dictionary*, 11th ed., s.v. "joy."
4. Richard Foster, *Celebration of Discipline*, 3rd ed. (New York: Harper Collins, 1998), p. 191.
5. *The Three-in-One Bible Reference Companion* (Nashville, TN: Thomas Nelson Publishers, 1982), s.v. "Hebrew feasts."
6. Wayne Jacobsen, *In My Father's Vineyard* (Dallas, TX: Word Publishing, 1997), p. 78.

EXPERIENCING
Spiritual
GROWTH

General Guidelines

1. Your role as a facilitator is to get women talking and discussing areas in their lives that are hindering them in their spiritual growth and personal identity.

2. Be mindful of the time. There are four sections in each study. Don't spend too much time on one section unless it is obvious that God is working in people's lives at a particular moment.

3. Emphasize that the group meeting is a time to encourage and share with one another. Stress the importance of confidentiality—what is shared stays within the group.

4. Fellowship time is very important in building small-group relationships. Providing beverages and light refreshments either before or after each session will encourage a time of informal fellowship.

5. Encourage journaling as it helps women apply what they are learning and stay focused during personal devotional time.

6. Most women lead very busy lives; respect group members by beginning and ending meetings on time.

7. Always begin and end the meetings with prayer. If your group is small, have the whole group pray together. If it is larger than 10 members, form groups of 2 to 4 to share and pray for one another.

   One suggestion is to assign prayer partners each week. Encourage each group member to complete a Prayer Request Form as she arrives. Members can select a prayer request before leaving the meeting and pray for that person during the week. Or two women can trade prayer requests and then pray for each other at the end of the meeting and throughout the week. Encourage the women to call their prayer partner at least once during the week.

8. Another highly valuable activity is to encourage the women to memorize the key verse each week.

9. Be prepared. Pray for your preparation and for the group members during the week. Don't let one person dominate the discussion. Ask God to help you draw out the quiet ones without putting them on the spot.

10. Enlist the help of other group members to provide refreshments, to greet the women, to lead a discussion group or to call absentees to encourage them, etc. Whatever you can do to involve the women will help bring them back each week.

11. Spend time each meeting worshiping God. This can be done either at the beginning or the end of the meeting.

How to Use the Material

Suggestions for Group Study

There are many ways that this study can be used in a group situation. The most common way is a small-group Bible study format. However, it can also be used in a women's Sunday School class. However you choose to use it, here are some general guidelines to follow for group study:

- Keep the group small—8 to 12 participants is probably the maximum for effective ministry, relationship building and discussion. If you have a larger group, form smaller groups for the discussion time, selecting a facilitator for each group.
- Ask the women to commit to regular attendance for the eight weeks of the study. Regular attendance is a key to building relationships and trust in a group.
- Whatever is discussed in the group meetings is to be held in strictest confidence among group members only.

Suggestions for Mentoring Relationships

This study also lends itself for use in relationships in which one woman mentors another woman. Women in particular are admonished in Scripture to train other women (see Titus 2:3-5).

- A mentoring relationship could be arranged through a system set up by a church or women's ministry.
- A less formal way to start a mentoring relationship is for a younger woman or new believer to take the initiative and approach an older or more spiritually mature woman who exemplifies the Christlike life and ask to meet with her on a regular basis. Or the reverse might be a more mature woman who approaches a younger woman or new believer to begin a mentoring relationship.
- When asked to mentor, someone might shy away, thinking that she could never do that because her own walk with the Lord is less than perfect. But just as we are commanded to disciple new believers, we must learn to disciple others to strengthen their walk. The Lord has promised to be "with you always" (Matthew 28:20).
- When you agree to mentor another woman, be prepared to learn as much or more than the woman you will mentor. You will both be blessed by the mentoring relationship built on the relationship you have together in the Lord.

There are additional helps for mentoring relationships or leading small groups in *The Focus on the Family Women's Ministry Guide*.

SESSION ONE—
DEMONSTRATING LOVE:
Fellowship

Before the Meeting

The following preparations should be made before each meeting:

1. Gather materials for making name tags (if the women do not already know each other and/or if you do not already know everyone's name). Also gather extra pens or pencils and Bibles to loan to anyone who may need them.
2. Make photocopies of the Prayer Request Form (available in *The Focus on*

the Family Women's Ministry Guide, chapter 9), or provide 3x5-inch index cards for recording requests.

3. Read through your own answers and mark the questions that you especially want to have the group discuss.

4. Make the necessary preparations for the ice-breaker activity you choose.

5. Have a whiteboard or poster board and the appropriate felt-tip pens available for the teaching time.

Ice Breakers

1. Distribute Prayer Request Forms, or index cards, and ask each woman to at least write down her name, even if she doesn't have a specific prayer request. This way, someone can pray for her during the upcoming week. This can be done each week. Just because we don't have a specific prayer request doesn't mean we don't need prayer!

2. **Option 1**—Introduce yourself and then share something unique about yourself. Have each woman in the group do likewise.

   Option 2—As the women arrive, hand each one a heart cut out of red, pink or white construction paper. Instruct the women to spend a few moments developing a definition of love and to write their definition on the heart with the felt-tip pens that you have provided. Once everyone has arrived, spend a few minutes reading the definitions and discussing how each one can be applied to genuine fellowship.

Discussion

1. **Everyday Woman**—Discuss the questions; then ask: **How might a woman's relational tendencies actually hinder her from true fellowship with others?**

2. **Eternal Wisdom**—Discuss why love is considered the root of all spiritual disciplines and the first characteristic of the fruit of the Spirit. Invite a volunteer to read 1 Corinthians 13; then begin the discussion of question 6 by asking one of the women to share her practical example of showing patience. Ask the woman closest to her to share her example of kindness. Continue around the room until all the characteristics of love have been discussed. As time allows, discuss questions 7 through 9, but especially focus on the third part of question 9.

3. **Enduring Hope**—Invite each woman in the group to share the spiritual gifts, abilities and passions she feels God has given her. Be prepared to answer any questions the women may have about the gifts listed in question 11, and have some reference materials you can recommend to the women who would like to learn more about spiritual gifts. Discuss how the gifts, abilities and passions represented by the women in the room fit together to help complete the Body of Christ.

> **Note:** Depending on the diversity and personalities of the women in your group and the denomination of your church, you may have differing opinions about the spiritual gifts. Be prepared to diffuse any "foolish controversies" (Titus 3:9).

4. **Everyday Life**—On a whiteboard or poster board, brainstorm ideas for meaningful fellowship as a group. Use the list on pages 16-17 to get you started, but don't stop there! Encourage the women to write down the ideas they generate on a piece of paper or on the inside cover of their Bible study to reference in the weeks to come. Be prepared to share the activities you have chosen for your one-week, one-month and three-month goals.

5. **Close in Prayer**—Ask a volunteer to close the group in prayer, thanking God for the beautiful and necessary gift of fellowship, and asking Him for the strength to love as He loves. Have each woman exchange her prayer request card with another member of the group and encourage the women to pray diligently for one another.

    Optional: Invite women who need prayer or counseling to stay after the meeting.

6. **Encourage Scripture Memory**—One very effective way to strengthen our relationship with God is to memorize His Word. Encourage the women to memorize the week's key verse or a verse from the lesson that was especially helpful for them. Provide an opportunity at each meeting for the women to recite their memory verses. *The Focus on the Family Women's Ministry Guide* contains additional information on encouraging Scripture memorization.

After the Meeting

1. **Evaluate**—Spend time evaluating the meeting's effectiveness (see *The Focus on the Family Women's Ministry Guide*, chapter 10, for an evaluation form).
2. **Encourage**—During the week, try to contact each woman (through phone calls, notes of encouragement, e-mails or instant messages) and welcome her to the study. Make yourself available to answer any questions or concerns the women may have and generally get to know them. If you have a large group, enlist the aid of some women in the group to contact others.
3. **Equip**—Complete the Bible study.
4. **Pray**—Prayerfully prepare for the next meeting, praying for each woman and your own preparation. Discuss with the Lord any apprehension, excitement or anything else that is on your mind regarding the Bible study material or the group members. If you feel inadequate or unprepared, ask for strength and insight. If you feel tired or burdened, ask for God's light yoke. Whatever it is you need, ask God for it. He will provide!

SESSION TWO—
EXEMPLIFYING GOODNESS:
Study

Before the Meeting

1. Make the usual preparations as listed on pages 87-88.
2. Make the necessary preparations for the ice-breaker activity you choose.
3. Gather the necessary materials for the teaching time.

Ice Breakers

1. Distribute Prayer Request Forms, or index cards, and remind the women to write down their names, even if they don't have any specific requests this week.
2. Invite a volunteer to lead the other women in reciting the memory verse.
3. Gather several hygiene products and food, such as hairspray, shampoo

or packaged foods, that have strange-sounding ingredients. Ask volunteers to read the ingredient labels to the group, and then to hypothesize what each ingredient is and what it does. Encourage the women to use their imaginations; the definitions they come up with need not have anything to do with the product! Once all the ingredient lists have been read, explain: **If reading your Bible feels a little like trying to make sense out of these ingredient lists, you are not alone. When you have trouble understanding the words of Scripture, it is much easier to give up and quit. That's why the tools described in this session are so important.**

Discussion

1. **Everyday Woman**—Discuss Jesus' words in Luke 6:44-45, and then ask a volunteer to read James 3:8-12. As a group, compare the two passages. How do they relate to one another? Explain: **The words that come out of our mouths are good indications of the state of our hearts. If you hear bitter, complaining, angry or untrue words coming from your mouth, it's time to assess the deeper issue.**

2. **Eternal Wisdom**—Ask volunteers to share their answers to question 2 and the third and fourth parts of question 3. Remind the group that we all struggle in this area and that no one should judge another. Be willing to share your own struggles and accomplishments in Bible study. Women appreciate transparency, so don't feel like you have to have it all together.

   Before the meeting, gather as many of the Bible study tools listed on pages 21-22 as possible. Have members form pairs, and assign each group one of the Bible study tools or one of the principles of hermeneutics. Depending on group size, each group may need to choose more than one. Invite a volunteer to give her favorite Scripture; then instruct the groups to learn as much as possible about that verse with the tool(s) that they have chosen. After 8 to 10 minutes, have each small group share what they found with the rest of the group.

3. **Enduring Hope**—Invite the small groups to discuss the questions in this section.

4. **Everyday Life**—Ask volunteers to share how their Bible study schedule has been going so far. Ask: **How have your times of study affected your desire to study? Your walk with the Lord? Your attitude toward**

your circumstances each day? Also discuss ways that Satan has and will try to distract us from regular times of study and how we can fight those attacks.

5. **Close in Prayer**—As you begin your time of prayer, read Psalm 19:7-11,14 aloud. Allow a few moments for silent prayer and meditation before closing. Thank God for His Word and for the tools that He has given us to learn from it. Collect the Prayer Request Forms and have each woman select one to pray for during the week.

   Optional: Invite women who need prayer or counseling to stay after the meeting.

After the Meeting

1. **Evaluate.**
2. **Encourage.** Call the women to encourage them to pray for their prayer partner. Also ask each woman to bring something to the meeting that reminds her of the simple pleasures of childhood (see the ice-breaker activity for session 3).
3. **Equip.**
4. **Pray.**

SESSION THREE—
EXPERIENCING PEACE:
Simplicity and Solitude

Before the Meeting

1. Make the usual preparations as listed on pages 87-88.
2. Make the necessary preparations for the ice-breaker activity.
3. Have a whiteboard and/or poster board and the appropriate felt-tip pens available for the teaching time.

Ice Breakers

1. Distribute Prayer Request Forms, or index cards, and encourage the women to write their names on the forms even if they don't have any specific requests this week. Encourage them to be specific about their requests.
2. Invite volunteers to recite the memory verse, or recite it as a group.
3. **Before the meeting,** call each woman and ask her to bring something to the meeting that reminds her of the simple pleasures of childhood. She could bring something as simple as a special doll with which she played make-believe or a favorite candy for the group to taste. Encourage the women to bring something that others can experience using taste, touch or smell. Once everyone has arrived, have the women show their items and briefly share.
4. Invite volunteers to share what they gained from their solitude appointments with God.

Discussion

1. **Everyday Woman**—Discuss question 1 and invite volunteers to share their answer to question 2.
2. **Eternal Wisdom**—Explain what it means to have ultimate peace and reconciliation with God through salvation. Be especially attentive to those who have questions about Christianity. Have the women form two groups; assign each group either the section on simplicity or the section on solitude to discuss for about 5 to 10 minutes. Then give each group a piece of poster board and several brightly colored felt-tip pens. Instruct the groups that they have 5 minutes to create a picture and/or word collage that depicts a way to find peace based on the topic their group discussed: simplicity or solitude. When the time is up, have one woman from each group share her group's artwork.
3. **Enduring Hope**—Discuss question 11 as a group. Invite a volunteer to share her answer to question 12.
4. **Everyday Life**—Invite volunteers who did not share at the beginning of the meeting to describe their experiences with their solitude appointments. Encourage the women to brainstorm ideas and suggestions for future times of solitude and for simplifying their lives.
5. **Close in Prayer**—Create an atmosphere of meditation (low lights, candles,

etc.) and allow the women to spend any remaining time in private prayer, Scripture reading and meditation. When the time is up, close the meeting in prayer. Have the women exchange prayer request cards with someone from their Eternal Wisdom activity. Encourage the women to call their prayer partner during the week to pray together over the phone.

Optional: Invite women who need prayer or counseling to stay after the meeting.

6. **Encourage Scripture Memory**—Encourage the women to memorize next week's key verse or a verse from the lesson that was especially helpful for them.

After the Meeting

1. **Evaluate.**
2. **Encourage.**
3. **Equip.**
4. **Pray.**

SESSION FOUR—
LIVING WITH PATIENCE AND GENTLENESS:
Submission

Before the Meeting

1. Make the usual preparations as listed on pages 87-88.
2. Make the necessary preparations for the ice-breaker activity.
3. Gather a basket or other container for the Close in Prayer section.

Ice Breakers

1. Distribute Prayer Request Forms, or index cards, and remind the women to write down their names, even if they don't have any specific requests this week.

2. Invite a volunteer to lead the other women in reciting the memory verse. Allow other volunteers to recite the verses from previous sessions.

3. Have the women form groups of three to five each, depending on your group size. Instruct each group to come up with a short skit—either funny or serious—illustrating someone who wants to get his or her own way. Have each group perform their skit for the remaining groups.

Discussion

1. **Everyday Woman**—Invite volunteers to share their answers to questions 1 and 2. Explain: **True submission can never be forced upon you, since it is a matter of the heart. It does not mean putting up with abuse or sexual harassment, or someone else's sinning.** As a group, brainstorm ways that submission plays an important role in our relationships with God (question 3).

2. **Eternal Wisdom**—Have the women return to the group they formed during the ice-breaker activity to discuss the definitions of "patience" and "gentleness" and their answers to questions 4 through 6.

3. **Enduring Hope**—With the whole group, read Philippians 2:5-11, and then discuss question 7. Invite one or two volunteers to share their answers to question 8.

4. **Everyday Life**—Invite the women to share their experiences with submitting their rights and benefits to others and choosing to display patience and gentleness this week. Be prepared to share your own experiences. Spend a few minutes emphasizing the importance of submitting our will to God instead of insisting that He do things our way.

5. **Close in Prayer**—Form a circle and have each woman who feels led to say a short sentence prayer praising God for being big enough to handle all of our frustrations and for sending His Son to be the ultimate example of submission. Place all the Prayer Request Forms, or index cards, in a basket and have the women take one as they leave.

    Optional: Invite women who need prayer or counseling to stay after the meeting.

6. **Encourage Scripture Memory**—Encourage the women to memorize the week's key verse or a verse from the lesson that was especially helpful for them.

After the Meeting

1. **Evaluate.**
2. **Encourage.**
3. **Equip.**
4. **Pray.**

SESSION FIVE—
DISPLAYING KINDNESS:
Service

Before the Meeting

1. Make the usual preparations as listed on pages 87-88.
2. Make the necessary preparations for the ice-breaker activity.
3. Gather the necessary materials for the teaching time.

Ice Breakers

1. Distribute Prayer Request Forms, or index cards, and remind the women to write down their names, even if they don't have any specific requests this week.
2. Invite a volunteer to lead the other women in reciting the memory verse. Allow other volunteers to recite the verses from the previous sessions.
3. Have each woman share her artwork or an element of her letter with the group. Remind the women that personal matters need not be shared, but only what will build up and minister to the group. Be prepared to share your "Words Full of Art" or "Words from the Heart" as well.

Discussion

1. **Everyday Woman**—Discuss questions 1 and 2. As the women share their answers to question 3, write their answers on a poster board or whiteboard. Discuss how the women's view of service may have changed as a result of this session.

2. **Eternal Wisdom**—Be sensitive to any questions the women may have about this section. Discuss question 4 and the paradox of Christ's royal hierarchy. Briefly overview the Serve Those Within Your Realm section before discussing question 7. Ask the women how the verses listed in question 7 correlate with serving those people God has put in their immediate view. Discuss questions 8 and 9, and then brainstorm ways that you might meet at least one of the needs as a group. Discuss question 10. Be sure the women understand why we can never gain salvation through doing acts of service or even being kind to others. Present the gospel message if appropriate for your group.

3. **Enduring Hope**—Invite volunteers to share their experiences with serving, even when they didn't feel like it (question 11). Be prepared to share your own struggles. Encourage the women that even the small acts of service and kindness toward others can have great impact for God's kingdom (question 13).

4. **Everyday Life—Before the meeting,** gather a small towel and a permanent felt-tip pen for each woman. **Note:** A washcloth, scrap of fabric or even a half-sheet of paper will also work. Dim the lights and read John 13:1-17 to the group. Hand each woman a towel and a marker. Say: **Though today we have no need to physically wash each other's feet, Christ set the example for us to serve one another in love. For the next several minutes, prayerfully consider practical ways that you can serve those God has placed in your life. Write those acts of service on the towel [paper] I have given you as a reminder to be a doer of the Word, not merely a hearer** (see James 1:22). Play a worship CD as the women pray and write.

5. **Close in Prayer**—After 3 to 5 minutes, close in prayer, thanking God for His Son's example of service and asking the Holy Spirit to continue to cultivate the fruit of kindness in each of your lives. Before the women leave, have them exchange Prayer Request Cards, or index cards, with someone with whom they have not yet exchanged prayer requests.

   Optional: Invite women who need prayer or counseling to stay after the meeting.

6. **Encourage Scripture Memory**—Encourage the women to memorize the week's key verse or a verse from the lesson that was especially helpful for them.

After the Meeting

1. **Evaluate.**
2. **Encourage.**
3. **Equip.**
4. **Pray.**

SESSION SIX—
WALKING IN FAITHFULNESS:
Integrity

Before the Meeting

1. Make the usual preparations as listed on pages 87-88.
2. Make the necessary preparations for the ice-breaker activity.
3. Gather a basket or other container for the Close in Prayer section.

Ice Breakers

1. Distribute Prayer Request Forms, or index cards, and remind the women to write down their names, even if they don't have any specific requests this week.
2. Invite a volunteer to lead the other women in reciting the memory verse. Invite volunteers to recite the verses from the previous sessions too.
3. Have the women form groups of four to five (if you have seven or fewer women, stay in one group). Give each group a dictionary, enough pens for each woman to have one, a large piece of paper and approximately two dozen 4¼ x 2¾-inch slips of paper (an 8½ x 11-inch sheet of paper makes 8 slips). The rules of play are similar to Balderdash. One person chooses a word from the dictionary that no one in the group is familiar with. Once she chooses a word, she will write down the correct definition on a slip of paper, while the other women each make up a definition. The woman with the dictionary will gather all the slips of paper in a small container, and then she will pull out at random the definitions, reading each one to the group. Each member of the group will then

choose which definition she believes is the correct one; the woman reading the definitions will mark each player's initials on the slip of paper corresponding with the definition she chose. Once the women have made their choices, the woman with the dictionary will read the correct definition, and the scorekeeper will tally up the scores.

Scoring: 1 point to each woman for every vote her phony definition receives; 2 points to each woman who chooses the correct definition; 3 points to the woman who reads the definitions if no one guesses the true meaning; 3 points to any woman who submits a definition that is very close to the correct meaning.

After each woman has had a chance to choose a word, have the scorekeeper announce the final scores to her group. Once all the groups have finished, announce the winners. You may choose to award small prizes. Discuss the implications of a game—though fun—that is based on telling lies. **How does it relate to the discipline of integrity?**

Discussion

1. **Everyday Woman**—Discuss the definitions of faithfulness and integrity. Invite two volunteers to share their answers to question 2.
2. **Eternal Wisdom—Before the meeting,** read through each of the five principles of integrity: pursue truth, be honest, love justice and mercy, show concern for others and develop a strong work ethic. As you discuss the questions, challenge the women to examine their hearts and allow God to reveal ways in which they can grow, whether they are new Christians or veteran saints.
3. **Enduring Hope**—Read the verses in question 15 and discuss the benefits. If there is time, invite one or two volunteers to share examples of how they have been blessed by God as a result of living in integrity. Allow them to share an example from their own life or from the life of someone they know or have read about.
4. **Everyday Life**—Have each woman in the group share one of her choose-your-own-adventure scenarios. These should be relatively short, but if you are running out of time, choose several volunteers to share theirs. Discuss—and/or laugh about—the implications of each outcome.
5. **Close in Prayer**—Have the women form a circle. After opening in prayer, encourage each woman to pray a sentence prayer beginning with the

words "Help me to be more . . . " and ending with a characteristic of faithfulness or integrity. After each woman has prayed, close in a final prayer. Place all the Prayer Request Forms, or index cards, in a basket and have each women take one as they leave.

Optional: Invite women who need prayer or counseling to stay after the meeting.

After the Meeting

1. **Evaluate.**
2. **Encourage.**
3. **Equip.**
4. **Pray.**

SESSION SEVEN—
PRACTICING SELF-CONTROL:
Fasting

Before the Meeting

1. Make the usual preparations as listed on pages 87-88.
2. Make the necessary preparations for the ice-breaker activity.
3. Make the necessary preparations for the teaching time.

Ice Breakers

1. Distribute Prayer Request Forms, or index cards, and remind the women to write down their names, even if they don't have any specific requests this week.
2. Invite a volunteer to lead the other women in reciting the memory verse. Invite several volunteers to recite the verses from the previous sessions.
3. There's nothing like an old-fashioned staring contest to fill a room with laughter! Have each woman find a partner and instruct them to stare at their partner until one of them smiles or laughs. The offender sits down. Then have the winners of each round find another partner. Continue

until you have one winner. You may choose to have a small prize for the winner. Discuss how this game is related (albeit loosely) to the self-control needed to refrain, or abstain, from physical pleasures.

Discussion

1. **Everyday Woman**—Discuss questions 1 and 2. Discuss some of the amazing pleasures generated by our five senses. To give contrast, describe a world in which we could not touch, taste, smell, see or hear anything. What would that sort of existence be like? Then describe a world in which there were no restraints on sensual pleasures. What would that sort of existence be like?

2. **Eternal Wisdom**—Discuss the questions. Then invite the women to share their fears or concerns regarding fasting. Answer their questions as best as you can and encourage them to do research on their own if they have questions that you cannot answer. Invite volunteers to share their experiences with fasting. The testimony of others is a powerful teaching tool!

3. **Enduring Hope**—Form groups of three or four women each to discuss questions 13 through 16.

4. **Everyday Life**—Have the women remain in small groups, and invite them to share their experiences of fasting or abstaining from other distractions that hinder them from focusing on God. Have group members pray for one another as they feel led.

5. **Close in Prayer**—Thank God for the many pleasures we enjoy every day and ask Him to give each of you the self-control needed to keep Him on the throne of your hearts. Before the women leave, instruct them to trade prayer request cards, or index cards, with someone for whom they have not prayed before.

   Optional: Invite women who need prayer or counseling to stay after the meeting.

After the Meeting

1. **Evaluate.**
2. **Encourage.** Call each woman to remind her to bring her Book of Celebration to share.

3. **Equip.**
4. **Pray.**

CULTIVATING JOY:
Celebration

Before the Meeting

1. Make the usual preparations as listed on pages 87-88.
2. Make the necessary preparations for the ice-breaker activity.
3. Make the necessary preparations for the teaching time.
4. Make photocopies of the Study Evaluation (see *The Focus on the Family Women's Ministry Guide*, chapter 9).

Ice Breakers

1. Distribute Prayer Request Forms, or index cards, and remind the women to write down their names, even if they don't have any specific requests this week.
2. Invite a volunteer to lead the other women in reciting the memory verse. Invite volunteers to recite the verses from all eight sessions. Be prepared with a gift for those who have memorized all eight verses.
3. Since this week's session is about joy and celebration, it is only fitting that the group session be a time to let down and enjoy! Before the women arrive, arrange to have group members bring a favorite dessert, game or party favor. Select several upbeat CDs to play during the meeting. You might even choose to decorate around a particular theme, such as a tropical paradise, a Mexican fiesta or a garden tea, depending on the time of year and your group's interests. As the women arrive, give each woman a self-adhesive name tag that reads "I'm full of joy because . . ." Instruct the women to ask each other why they are full of joy and to be prepared to answer other questions. Play music and offer the treats the women brought while they mingle.

Discussion

1. **Everyday Woman**—Rather than an extensive teaching time, this session should be focused on celebration. You may ask the women if they have any questions regarding the lesson, or briefly review the concepts, but spend more time simply discussing the reasons we have to celebrate and how we can plan times of celebration and remembrance.

2. The women should have brought their Books of Celebration to the meeting. Spend time discussing what each woman included—or plans to include—in her book.

   Option: Have supplies ready to create a Book of Celebration specific to your group. Have each woman create a page highlighting things she is thankful for or can rejoice about because of her involvement in the group. Collect the pages and keep them in a three-ring binder to revisit often.

3. Invite volunteers to share ways that they have grown through the course of this study. Allow ample time for this activity, as the main goal of today's session is to reflect on the ways each woman has grown.

4. Spend any remaining time playing games, singing or reading psalms of joy together.

5. **Close in Prayer**—Invite the women to thank the Lord for the many things He has taught them in the past several weeks about spiritual disciplines and the fruit of the Spirit. You may also choose to pray a special blessing on each woman present.

After the Meeting

1. **Evaluate**—Distribute the Study Evaluation forms for members to take home with them. Share about the importance of feedback, and ask members to take the time this week to write their review of the group meetings and then return them to you.

2. **Encourage**—Contact each woman during the week to invite her to the next Focus on the Family Women's Bible study.